Your
Horoscope
2021

....

Sagittarius

23 November – 21 December

igloobooks

Published in 2020
by Igloo Books Ltd
Cottage Farm
Sywell
NN6 0BJ
www.igloobooks.com

0820 001
2 4 6 8 10 9 7 5 3 1
ISBN 978-1-83852-322-0

Written by Belinda Campbell and Denise Evans

Cover design by Simon Parker
Edited by Bobby Newlyn-Jones

Printed and manufactured in China

CONTENTS

INTRODUCTION
. . . .

This 15-month guide has been designed and written to give a concise and accessible insight into both the nature of your star sign and the year ahead. Divided into two main sections, the first section of this guide will give you an overview of your character in order to help you understand how you think, perceive the world and interact with others and – perhaps just as importantly – why. You'll soon see that your zodiac sign is not just affected by a few stars in the sky, but by planets, elements, and a whole host of other factors, too.

The second section of this guide is made up of daily forecasts. Use these to increase your awareness of what might appear on your horizon so that you're better equipped to deal with the days ahead. While this should never be used to dictate your life, it can be useful to see how your energies might be affected or influenced, which in turn can help you prepare for what life might throw your way.

By the end of these 15 months, these two sections should have given you a deeper understanding and awareness of yourself and, in turn, the world around you. There are never any definite certainties, but with an open mind you will find guidance for what might be, and learn to take more control of your own destiny.

THE CHARACTER OF THE ARCHER

....

A sign that loves to wonder and wander, Sagittarians are the explorers of the zodiac, both in their minds and around the globe. Born in the ninth house of the zodiac calendar that signifies growth, progress for the sake of progress is not what this sign stands for, as the journey itself will be important to this meaningful traveller, not just the destination. The Sagittarian's quest for adventure, be it intellectual or physical, can be unquenchable because their element, fire, needs constantly fuelling to keep its flames burning bright. This sign can certainly shine brighter than most, ruled by the largest and third brightest planet in the sky. Named after the Roman ruler of gods, Jupiter makes sure that Sagittarians live with confidence and luck on their side; or perhaps it's not luck, but the hand of a higher being, as this sign can be highly spiritual or religious. Whether it's the good fortune of wealth, happiness, family, or faith this sunny sign will find something in their life that makes them feel lucky to be alive.

Born at the end of autumn, Sagittarians are mutable and are perhaps the most open-minded to change of all the signs. Openness can breed honesty, which is perhaps why Sagittarians are commonly known as the zodiac's truth-tellers. Honesty is this sign's best policy, but their blunt delivery can sometimes need finessing. The Centaur Archer that symbolises Sagittarius can be an indicator of this sign's daring attitude and physical strength. With a positive energy that embraces physical challenges, Sagittarians can make fearless sports figures, like Eddie the Eagle with his record-breaking ski stunts. Above all, this sign can be an icon of inspiration, from Britney Spears to Winston Churchill, and at their core Sagittarians can motivate, bring joy, and encourage positive change.

THE CENTAUR ARCHER

Mind of a man and body of a beast, the mythological symbol of the Centaur is one of the dual signs in the zodiac. As with any dual sign, like Gemini's twins and Pisces' two fishes, there are usually two sides to them. With Sagittarians it is usually divided as their Centaur symbol suggests, by the mind and body. This sign is full of influential thinkers from William Blake to daring athletic personalities like Bruce Lee (who was also a known philosopher). The Archer signifies many of a Sagittarian's qualities: strong, daring, but perhaps none more so than this optimistic sign's ability to always look to the future. Sagittarians' aim can strike true first time, with the luck of the ruling planet Jupiter, or can dramatically miss. But fail or succeed, this hopeful sign is the embodiment of not giving up. The Archer can be dangerous, so risk-taking is usually common for many Sagittarians. As with any wild animal, the Centaur can at times feel restless, especially if they feel caged in any way. Sagittarians need to roam freely both in the mind and body to achieve their fullest potential.

JUPITER

Ruled by the largest planet in the sky, Sagittarians are hard to miss. They are watched over by Jupiter, the ruler of the gods in Roman mythology, who ruled over the sky and was usually depicted holding his trident of lightening. For most Sagittarians, the sky's the limit and they will live their lives with optimism and the desire to broaden their horizons. The sky is an important symbol in many religions and soul-searching Sagittarians may have a strong spiritual or religious faith. Jupiter is the fastest spinning planet in the solar system, resulting in it having the shortest days of all the planets, which perhaps explains Sagittarians' restlessness and desire to live each minute to its fullest. Jupiter is well known for having a red spot, which we now know to be a continuously raging storm. Whilst Sagittarians don't often lose their temper, this red spot on their ruling planet could be an indicator that when this sign is angry, it will be visible for everyone to see. Jupiter is associated with good luck, and with a daring fire sign like Sagittarius, fortune is likely to favour this brave sign.

ELEMENTS, MODES AND POLARITIES

Each sign is made up of a unique combination of three defining groups: elements, modes and polarities. Each of these defining parts can manifest themselves in good and bad ways and none should be seen to be a positive or a negative – including the polarities! Just like a jigsaw puzzle, piecing these groups together can help illuminate why each sign has certain characteristics and help us to find a balance.

ELEMENTS

Fire: Dynamic and adventurous, signs with fire in them can be extroverted. Others are naturally drawn to them because of the positive light they give off, as well as their high levels of energy and confidence.

Earth: Signs with the earth element are steady and driven with their ambitions. They make for a solid friend, parent or partner due to their grounded influence and nurturing nature.

Air: The invisible element that influences each of the other elements significantly, air signs will provide much-needed perspective to others with their fair thinking, verbal skills and key ideas.

Water: Warm in the shallows and freezing as ice. This mysterious element is essential to the growth of everything around it, through its emotional depth and empathy.

MODES

Cardinal: Pioneers of the calendar, cardinal signs jump-start each season and are the energetic go-getters.

Fixed: Marking the middle of the calendar, fixed signs firmly denote and value steadiness and reliability.

Mutable: As the seasons end, the mutable signs adapt and give themselves over gladly to the promise of change.

POLARITIES

Positive: Typically extroverted, positive signs take physical action and embrace outside stimulus in their life.

Negative: Usually introverted, negative signs value emotional development and experiencing life from the inside out.

SAGITTARIANS IN BRIEF

The table below shows the key attributes of Sagittarians. Use it for quick reference and to understand more about this fascinating sign.

SYMBOL	RULING PLANET	MODE	ELEMENT	HOUSE
↗	♃	△·	△	IX
The Centaur Archer	Jupiter	Mutable	Fire	Ninth

COLOUR	BODY PART	POLARITY	GENDER	POLAR SIGN
		⊕	♂	II
Purple	Hips, Thighs, Liver	Positive	Masculine	Gemini

ROMANTIC RELATIONSHIPS

. . . .

Like a moth to the flame, this fire sign draws lovers into its inviting light purely by being its dynamic and sociable Sagittarian self. Confident Sagittarians are not shy of taking the lead and braving it alone, but if they can find a partner to take on their endless journeys then they can experience their greatest adventures yet. A relationship that does not compromise their individuality in any way will be essential: a Sagittarian will not happily sacrifice their own dreams for others, like, for example, Pisceans often do. They will also abhor any signs of possessiveness from their partner, so Scorpio or Taurus lovers could be problematic. Sagittarians may have trouble committing to the one partner if they feel that the relationship is binding their freedom in any way. Learning to share their time and the art of compromising will be two tricky areas in love that this sign may need to work harder at.

With free-roaming Sagittarians, the grass can have a habit of always looking greener and they may be inclined to eagerly wander from one relationship to another. If they want to find a long-lasting love that keeps the passions of their fire element burning night after night, then finding a like-minded intellectual or outdoorsy explorer to share their life with will be key. Air signs will not only keep this fire sign burning, they are also associated with the mind and ideas so could make ideal partners for a Sagittarian looking for mental stimulation from their partner. A stimulating spouse is a must, as is finding common interests, which for this positive sign may mean adventures in the great outdoors like holidays spent wild camping and roasting marshmallows on a campfire. A sign that has a matching positive energy will have a good chance of keeping up physically with this wild Centaur. Fundamentally, this forward-thinking Archer could benefit most from an open-minded partner with whom they can see a future.

ARIES: COMPATIBILITY 5/5

If Aries gets struck by one of Sagittarius' arrows it will be a sure sign of Cupid's work. This couple's compatibility is high due to their matching positivity and lively personalities. Aries may have finally found their true match in risk-taking Sagittarius. With a shared love of travel, there's unlikely to be any Sagittarius adventure that the Aries would pass up on. These two are go-getters and if they can find shared interests then this partnership is an ideal match of two pioneering signs, the Ram and Centaur happily galloping side by side.

TAURUS: COMPATIBILITY 2/5

Sagittarius is ruled by the planet Jupiter which is associated with luck, something that a Taurus doesn't always believe in, valuing hard work more. Whilst a Sagittarian values new experiences, Taureans can prefer the comforts of what they know. The biggest struggle that this fire and earth couple may have is Sagittarius' need for freedom and Taurus' tendency towards possessiveness with their partners. A claustrophobic atmosphere should be avoided, and freedom generously given in this relationship. Learn from each other, admire the faster gallop of the Centaur and equally appreciate the steady plod of the Bull.

GEMINI: COMPATIBILITY 5/5

'I love you just the way you are,' could be the vows of strongly independent signs Sagittarius and Gemini. Despite being both mutable signs that are open to adapt, there is unlikely to be anything about this match that either partner will want to change about the other. Being opposite signs on the zodiac calendar, the bond between Sagittarius and Gemini is usually going to be unique. For a sign that can become easily bored like Gemini, the adventurous Sagittarian is a perfect fit and will ensure this couple have endless days of love and fun ahead of them.

CANCER: COMPATIBILITY 1/5

The homebody Cancer might end up feeling lost with the adventuring wanderer that is Sagittarius. Daring Sagittarians can help bring out a worldlier side to Cancerians and teach them that their sense of community can stretch larger than the end of their road. With Cancer, the roaming Sagittarius can learn the benefits of settling down in a loving relationship. These two have contrasting masculine and feminine energies that can complement each other greatly if their differences are nurtured rather than discouraged. Give each other plenty of room to be and reap the many rewards from when opposites attract.

LEO: COMPATIBILITY 4/5

With two fire signs like adventurous Sagittarius and spontaneous Leo, theirs is a love that will surely spark with excitement. Here is a couple that should keep their passports to hand as either one is likely to plan a surprise romantic getaway for the other with little or no notice. Leo and Sagittarius match each other with their positive energies and are probably the dynamic couple that is at the top of every party invite list. The philosophical Sagittarius and purpose-led Leo can share a powerful bond whose influence could be felt well beyond them.

VIRGO: COMPATIBILITY 2/5

Whilst the outdoorsy Sagittarius and earth sign Virgo both have a strong love for being outside in nature, they have some serious core differences, such as Virgo's love for routine and Sagittarians' dislike of the same; so these two lovers may have their work cut out for them. The wild Centaur can sometimes feel too reckless for the over-thinking Virgo as they bolt heart-first after their goals, whilst a Sagittarian might feel that the Virgoan's overactive mind is slowing them down. Find some common ground, and this mutable pair could experience an honest and thought-provoking relationship.

LIBRA: COMPATIBILITY 4/5

The good fortune of Sagittarius' Jupiter and the love of Libra's Venus could make these two lucky in love together. Fire sign Sagittarius and air sign Libra are sure to get each other hot under the collar with their complimentary elements helping to keep their passions burning. Both high energy positive signs, they should have no problem keeping up with each other's packed social schedules and will share plenty of adventures. The tactful Libra and sometimes blunt Sagittarius could clash if their ideas of commitment don't match, but they have a good chance of working out their differences and happily moving forward together.

SCORPIO: COMPATIBILITY 2/5

Sagittarius and Scorpio can have a daring partnership: whether their gamble on each other pays off is another thing entirely. The adventurous Sagittarian will help expand Scorpio's horizons and appeal to their brave side, whilst Scorpio's fixed attitude can teach the flaky Sagittarian to stay motivated and see things through. The love of Scorpio can be all encompassing and the worst thing for a Sagittarian is for them to feel like their partner is at all possessive. This is definitely not a boring love, but flexibility and growth are both key for these two getting the most out of the relationship.

SAGITTARIUS: COMPATIBILITY 4/5

An honest and awe-inspiring couple, these two lively Sagittarian intellects can have a fiery love. If any couple stood a chance with making a long-distance relationship work, it would be these two independent spirits. Two Sagittarian lovers will understand the importance of each other's independence so will be accustomed to giving each other as much breathing space as necessary. Their mutable natures make them flexible and ready for big changes in the relationship, whether it's moving to another country or starting a family. This is a pair that can inspire, spark, and dare one another to reach the highest of heights.

CAPRICORN: COMPATIBILITY 2/5

A materialist Capricorn and dazzling Sagittarius can both be guilty of feeling a little superior, which won't do in a partnership, especially when these two can have such different approaches to life. The rational Capricorn may be fearful of going to daring heights with their lively Sagittarius partner but if they are open to Sagittarius' optimism, they could learn to love more bravely. Sagittarius may feel constrained by Capricorn's constant reminder that actions have consequences, but looking before they leap could be a vital lesson for a Capricorn to teach their Sagittarian partner. The key to their happiness will be embracing each other's opposites.

AQUARIUS: COMPATIBILITY 4/5

Placed two apart on the zodiac calendar, the positive energies
of an Aquarian and Sagittarian can be a complementary
and exciting love match. The thrilling ideas of a Sagittarius
combined with the Aquarian's independent thinking can
mean that these stimulating spouses will have plenty to talk
about. The fire in Sagittarius brings an enthusiastic energy
to the relationship and the fixed mode of Aquarius can help
provide a focus to their ideas and bring them to fruition.
Communal-minded Aquarius and sociable Sagittarius will
likely be at the heart of their shared communities and bring
great meaning to each other's lives.

PISCES: COMPATIBILITY 3/5

The roaming Sagittarius and the escapist Pisces could end
up blissfully running off into the sunset together if they can
learn from each other's differences. Both ruled by Jupiter,
these two may indeed have been lucky to find one another.
Jupiter gives Sagittarians and Pisceans a zest for life and their
shared mutable modes will make their relationship open to
continuous growth and change. Pisceans can lack the active
side that many fire signs have, whilst Sagittarians can lack
compassion which could lead to clashes with this sensitive
water sign. Focus on common interests and this deep pair
could go far.

FAMILY AND FRIENDS

Friends and family of a Sagittarian should be ready to get taken on a journey. Whether it's road-tripping down Route 66 or escaping to a meditation retreat, a Sagittarian can inspire both physical journeys and mental ones, as their duality of the Centaur (half man, half horse) suggests. Yoga mat at the ready, water sign and spiritual Piscean friends or family members can make the perfect partner to go in search of higher meaning and mindful enlightenment with. For more physical adventures, the active fire sign of Aries will rise to a sporty Sagittarian's challenge and race them to the top of any mountain. It's not all about the thrill of life that urges this sign on in their constant state of exploration: Sagittarians enjoy finding meaning in the world and what they do. As the charitable Sagittarian races over the marathon finishing line in their banana costume, their philanthropic Cancerian friends and family members are sure to be there cheering and offering their generous support.

A Sagittarian is a known truth-teller and sometimes their candid words of advice can be felt deeply by their sensitive family and friends. Whilst honesty is an admirable quality, the way in which Sagittarians deliver their wise words to their loved ones may need some work. Scorpio is a daring friend that may be close to a Sagittarian, and whilst the Scorpion is made of hardy stuff, any water sign has a sensitive soul that the blunt words of a Sagittarian should be wary of damaging if they want to hold on to their friendships. Expert communicator Gemini and diplomatic Libra may be able to help their Sagittarian friend word things in a more tactful way so that their words inspire rather than injure. The famous writer and Sagittarius Dale Carnegie, who wrote How to Win Friends and Influence People, shows just how influential the voice of a Sagittarian can be when delivered in a positive way.

FAMILY AND FRIENDS

Should the studious Sagittarius wish to start their own family, their love for learning will no doubt be something that they will want to pass on to their children. Sagittarians can make wonderful teachers, whether it's teaching their child to throw a ball or learn a new language; for the travelling Sagittarian, they may decide to bring their children up in a foreign country to truly broaden their horizons and give them their first taste of adventure. The Archer looks to the future, and as a parent the future of their children could be of utmost importance to this sign; planning which schools they will attend, enrolling them in sports clubs, teaching them piano may all be things that the forward-thinking Sagittarian partner thinks about early on as they encourage their child to explore their full potential. As their children grow up, and even when they become adults, the Sagittarius parent will continue to try and challenge their children and impart their wisdom.

MONEY AND CAREERS

Being a certain star sign will not dictate the type of career that you have, although the characteristics that fall under each sign could help you identify the areas in which you could potentially thrive. Conversely, to succeed in the workplace, it is just as important to understand what you are good at as it is to know what you are less brilliant at so that you can see the areas in which you will need to perhaps work harder to achieve your career and financial goals.

Sagittarians understand the preciousness of time, remember Jupiter has the shortest days of all the planets, so they might not work well with colleagues prone to dithering. As a boss, Sagittarians can be inspiring, but they can also be preachy, impatient and downright mean in their critique. Sagittarians should try to appreciate that not everyone works at the same fast pace as them (Virgos especially like taking their time over projects) and what feels obvious to them sometimes needs to be pointed out to others. Sagittarians can continue to inspire by showing compassion and patience and always offering to help those that need help.

Clear career paths such as studying law, going to film-making school, or practising to become a singer could suit the Archer who has a clear aim in life. Caged within the confines of an office might not suit all Sagittarians, so finding a career that has travel prospects could appeal to this wild traveller. This highly sociable sign may enjoy a career that allows them to speak to the masses, whether it's as an academic lecturer that uses their intellect or a spiritual or religious leader that brings meaning to life. The most influential Sagittarians in their professional field, such as Steven Spielberg, Jimi Hendrix or Taylor Swift, are well loved because they have followed their dreams and help to inspire others to do the same.

The thrill-seeking Sagittarian may need to keep their wild spending in check and always use their heads when looking to invest or gamble their money, especially if they don't have endless funds to play with. Sagittarians may be interested in more high-risk investments but, being born in the ninth house of progression, they are also a fan of seeing things grow so a more secure financial venture could bring equal satisfaction as they are more likely to see their money grow steadily but surely. If lucky Jupiter is shining down on them, Sagittarians may find themselves galloping to the races with an uncanny ability to pick out the strongest horses thanks to their inner Centaur.

HEALTH AND WELLBEING

Whilst Sagittarians don't often lose their temper, the red tempestuous spot that storms constantly on their ruling planet of Jupiter can be an indicator of the public outbursts that this sign can be capable of. Sagittarian Britney Spears was known only for her singing and sunny southern charm until she was hounded by the paparazzi to the brink of a breakdown. Britney in 2007 is an extreme example of when a Sagittarian dramatically loses their nerve in public. The positivity of Sagittarians is a noble quality, however, this dual sign has ups and downs just like the rest of the world and cannot be expected to be all smiles. Learning how to release any upset in a positive way, whether it be through attending therapy, writing poetry, or trying out a boxercise class, is important for any sign and something that Sagittarians should not neglect.

For anyone that is prone to taking risks, they understand that danger is an inevitable part of the thrill. For Sagittarians, their physical activities may include hazardous sports like mountaineering or even being a stunt double. If risk is part of a Sagittarian's daily job or an aspect of their hobby, this sign may need to take extra care of their physical and mental health so that their body and mind can endure the extra stresses put upon it. Practising yoga and meditation could be helpful exercises for bringing strength and calmness to their action-packed life. If a Sagittarian is too restless for yoga, channelling the Archer in them could be a perfect way of satisfying their need for danger in the safety of a controlled environment of an archery class.

HEALTH AND WELLBEING

Sagittarians are usually sociable creatures and the life and soul of any party, which might have them out drinking and partying regularly. Over-indulging can be a problem for some born under this sign and with the liver being one of the parts of the body that Sagittarians are associated with, hangovers could be particularly unpleasant for them, or at least that might be their excuse for staying in bed. Keeping a broad variety of friends will help a Sagittarian's social calendar have a healthier balance of partying and relaxation time. The invite for tea at a Taurean's house is just as important as the Leo friend that always has tickets for premiers or nightclub openings.

For Sagittarians that feel the Centaur running strongly inside of them, spending time outdoors will be of huge importance to their physical and mental health. For a sign that is constantly on the move like wildfire, taking a slow walk to soak up the wonders of Mother Nature could help soothe their racing mind. For city Sagittarians, reading their book in a park or signing up for an outdoor bootcamp class could help bring them back to earth. Some Sagittarians may find that they have an affinity with horses and that the feeling of countryside air rushing past their cheeks gives them the greatest pleasure. If this sign is so inclined, horse riding will have the double benefit of bringing them joy and a level of fitness.

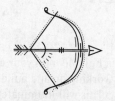

Sagittarius

DAILY FORECASTS
for 2020

OCTOBER

. . . .

Thursday 1st

October begins with a Full Moon in your creative sector.
What you have been working on and building may well
come to fruition now. This will illuminate how strong and
determined you have been all year. Love affairs may come
back into the light. Keep up with the self-expression, you
are doing well Sagittarius.

Friday 2nd

Venus now enters your career sector and will infuse the
workplace with love and harmony. As she is also the ruler
of money, this will give your finances a boost. You may also
find that your willingness to serve is at peace with your own
agendas now. Enjoy Venus' influence here.

Saturday 3rd

The Moon enters your sector of health and duty. She makes a
helpful connection to Venus and all the Venus issues of love,
harmony, peace and money will affect your daily schedule. You
may take some time for yourself now and not feel guilty about it.

Sunday 4th

Today will bring up a potentially difficult situation. The Moon sits
on top of Uranus the disruptor and is also opposite motormouth
Mercury in your deep, hidden parts. Mercury may find something
that makes you very uncomfortable. This has come up for healing
now, don't be afraid of your own shadow.

Monday 5th

Breathe! Pluto is direct. He is the last of the planets blocking your progress with money to go forward again. You will notice that things in this area will pick up enormously now. The passing Moon in your duties sector gives her blessing to all three and you are more emotionally stable.

Tuesday 6th

You can have a welcome break today and spend time with a lover or your inner lover. Conversations are stimulating and upbeat now that the heavyweights are facing forward. This influence can make you laugh and get your joy for life back again. Simply have light-hearted connections today.

Wednesday 7th

There is a chance that someone may knock you off your happy place today. This could be more stuff from your subconscious rising up and making itself known. You must learn that these moments are happening for you to heal your wounds and let your shadow see the light.

Thursday 8th

The Moon drifts into your sex, death and rebirth sector. What have you learned regarding hiding your feelings? You could feel exposed today as a lover or partner wants to probe deeper than you would like. Defence isn't necessary if you can just learn to trust and open up.

Friday 9th

Retrograde Mars is sulking in your creative sector. There may be issues of control now. Someone could be acting out on you and trying to push an issue that they feel is important. Use your communication skills to control the situation. Don't manipulate. Stay calm and objective.

Saturday 10th

The Moon sits opposite your money sector. You might be thinking about finances that you share with another person. Investments seem like a good idea but you may not want to indulge now that you have some control back with your money and resources. Put this away for another time.

Sunday 11th

When the Moon enters your travel sector, you usually feel brave and adventurous. Today she makes unhappy connections which could rock your boat. You can be knocked off a pedestal now and feel the bruises on your ego. Don't make a song and dance or you will be seen as a fool.

Monday 12th

You begin to wonder where your passion for being unique has led you. Higher education and travel have always interested you and set you apart from friends and family members but now you feel that you are left alone. Is there no-one who is on your wavelength?

Tuesday 13th

The Sun sits opposite retrograde Mars and laughs at the tantrums he is having. Is this you having a meltdown and acting like a spoilt child? Mercury goes retrograde tomorrow so use this energy to get all your devices backed up. Double check travel plans now.

Wednesday 14th

Mercury retrograde begins. This will be a difficult one for you because as you know, he is excavating your psyche right now and has already made you feel uncomfortable. Venus and the Moon sit together making work a happy place to be. Meditate upon this for a moment. Find your self-worth.

Thursday 15th

There could be power struggles within your social network today. Who's the boss? People may want to drag you down into an abyss but this is nothing to do with you so stay away from the edge. The Moon enters this sector and you feel the need to mediate the situation.

Friday 16th

Today there is a New Moon in your social sector. You may have noticed that some friends have disappeared from your life. These may have only been online acquaintances. This Moon asks that you set intentions around the groups you belong to. Not all are worth your time.

Saturday 17th

You may be deeply wounded. The Moon sits on Mercury and both are opposite Uranus. This means that whatever Mercury has found, maybe an old wound or something you have refused to acknowledge will surface. Don't pick at an old scab, give it the air it needs to heal.

Sunday 18th

You have a chance to learn a hard lesson. Saturn is in contact with the Sun and these tend to show where authority figures influence you. This can make you rebellious or humble. Maybe it is you that is the authority and you question your leadership.

Monday 19th

Jupiter is getting messages from both Venus and Mars. It's likely that there will be some exaggeration of points of view now. Women will win the day as Venus has a nice connection whereas men are being put in their places. Things could get out of hand.

Tuesday 20th

You may be pulled in two different directions now. The Moon in your sign is asking you to dream up a do-able vision of your future. Thoughts of the past make you lack the confidence to go after your goals. Meanwhile, Mercury is asking that you watch what you say.

Wednesday 21st

The lady boss Venus is sweet-talking the man boss. Her feminine charms can come in useful in the workplace now. If there is something you want to change, the chances are that under this influence you make it happen. Don't be afraid to use gentle persuasion.

Thursday 22nd

The Sun now moves into your dreams sector and will light up the dark areas for Mercury to find his way around. You feel more optimistic about being able to sort out your worries as the Moon passes through your money sector unimpeded by retrograde planets.

Friday 23rd

Your communications sector may see you making short trips. All is good in the workplace and you are getting the job done with limited pressure. You may feel some anxiety as the Moon connects with retrograde Mercury. This could mean that you need to repeat a conversation you have had recently.

Saturday 24th

Today you may get more responsibility in the workplace. You have been appraised and found to be a valuable member of the team. This could be a welcome surprise and can help you out with your financial difficulties. Take it on board, you deserve it.

Sunday 25th

Mercury is nowhere to be found. His excavation of your psyche has halted and you feel this. You could be wondering what he is up to, what will be his next move. Be assured that he is doing his best to make you feel comfortable with the darkness within. He is, after all, mining for gold.

Monday 26th

There will be pleasant surprises coming your way. An easy-going family event warms your heart and you feel good with your tribe today. Chatter is easy and people around you show their appreciation of who you are as an individual within the family group. Enjoy this day.

Tuesday 27th

Family merges and pulls together now. The Moon is sitting with Neptune who can dissolve boundaries. This isn't always a good thing but today it means that family connections are important and nurturing. Your urge to stand alone is put to one side and you become part of the clan.

Wednesday 28th

Today is like a bookend day where you can either feel hemmed in or supported. Venus enters your social sector while Mercury retrogrades back into it. There may be some tension with friends. Your social calendar could be full to brimming now and you may not have time for everyone.

Thursday 29th

The Moon meets a weary Mars in your creative sector. Your artistic pursuits have been paused for a while and you get the itch to start them back up again. Unfortunately, you don't have the energy right now. These will still be here for you when Mars turns direct again.

Friday 30th

Mundane activities keep you happy. You go along with your day, do the nine to five and have room left over for your own needs. This is the type of day which satisfies you. No tension, time for everything and chores all finished. Well done.

Saturday 31st

There's a Blue Moon in your health and duties sector. This is a second Full Moon in a calendar month. This Moon sits on top of Uranus so expect the unexpected today and join in any Halloween parties going on. Enjoy the thrill of this fun holiday.

NOVEMBER

. . . .

Sunday 1st

With all the recent exploration in your dreams sector, you may now be feeling the need for a spiritual connection. You look for a teacher or a guru. Revelations from deep within you have come up and might be earth-shattering but you now know what to do with them.

Monday 2nd

The Moon moves into your relationship sector and makes a helpful connection to Saturn. Talking with a partner or an influential person will give you some new ideas. The world is bigger than you think and there are options available to you that may have not been visible before now.

Tuesday 3rd

Conversations with both sexes can help you form an impression of how you relate to people. You will understand how your communication style differs whether it is a man or a woman you are talking to. What do you learn from this? Which sex can teach you the most?

Wednesday 4th

Mercury goes direct. He will once more travel over the last degrees of your social sector and this too can help you see how you relate. Close friends see one side of you, online friends another. You have a knack of adopting different personas depending on who you are interacting with.

Thursday 5th

You may feel vulnerable. Your recent discoveries into the relating styles you use have made you feel uncertain about yourself. You would rather stay at home in your own little world. Occult or taboo subjects interest you but you aren't about to open up about this just yet.

Friday 6th

The Moon is making a tense connection to Mars and you may feel drained of energy. Nothing is getting done regarding your creative pursuits or expressing yourself right now. This could be frustrating you. Begrudgingly, you put these aside in favour of more pressing matters. You might feel that no-one is listening.

Saturday 7th

As the Moon enters your travel sector, you wish to get yourself out there and be seen and heard. This can make you rather pushy and no-one likes a show-off. You must learn to just be yourself you are perfect as you are. You are a unique individual.

Sunday 8th

You will be as stubborn as an ox now. Your opinion is the only right one and no other will do. You may argue with authority figures. You have a right to your opinion but so does everyone else. Don't voice yours unless you are prepared to hear others.

Monday 9th

A battle of the sexes will occur. This could also be a conflict between yourself and another. The Moon is in your work sector so be careful not to upset the boss now. There is an 'us' and 'them' battle going on. Which side are you on?

Tuesday 10th

Mercury hangs around in the last degree of your social sector. He has been there twice before in recent days so take this as a warning. There is something you need to deal with regarding your associates. Put something right or apologise now before it's too late and you lose a friend.

Wednesday 11th

Once again the winged messenger heads for your dreams sector. This area deals with your solitude and how you manage that. You may have had enough of this lately and resort to mind-numbing substances such as drugs or alcohol. Try chocolate and trash TV instead.

Thursday 12th

There are lovely connections happening in the sky, so make the most of them while they're here. You feel an emotional pull toward friendship groups. Venus adds her charm and restores harmony. Any kind of transformation you would like to make is favoured now by a Jupiter and Pluto meet-up in your finance sector.

Friday 13th

Your emotions are intense now. You may begin to see the benefit of Mercury's digging around. The Moon enters your dreams sector and once more you may want to self-soothe with substances. If you choose to do this, the Jupiter and Pluto meet-up can make this get out of control.

Saturday 14th

You may feel extremely tired. Mars is turning around and will go direct again. Although this is good news, you may feel this like a stone attached to your ankles. Get through the day and you will see the change in your energy. Things you're passionate about will be re-started.

Sunday 15th

A New Moon in your dreams sector gives you the chance to firmly make resolutions regarding your shadow side. Mercury has given you the lead and now you must make it into gold. There may be a struggle with women today. Don't try to control others now.

Monday 16th

Venus calls the shots and dances around your social sector trying to get her own way. You or someone around you could be acting like a stroppy child. An elder will come along and cut you, or the stroppy child down to size. Stop being a drama queen.

Tuesday 17th

Be careful with your words. Mercury is sitting opposite
Uranus and this placement usually means that words spoken
can be hurtful. This may also mean that you have a fantastic
idea that has come from nowhere. If you have an 'aha'
moment, use it wisely.

Wednesday 18th

Actions and emotions are at odds. Emotionally, you're consumed
with thoughts about finances and what you own. However, your
actions speak otherwise and you could be making a spontaneous
purchase. Use your restless energy to make something. Be proud
that your enthusiasm is back but don't abuse it.

Thursday 19th

The Moon passes over your money sector. Things don't look
as bad as they have done all year. You have learned more
about taking responsibility for yourself and your spending.
A more mature you has emerged which makes you proud.
Don't undo all the hard work.

Friday 20th

Your communications sector gets a hit and you will find that
you just cannot say right for saying wrong. You put your foot
in your mouth with most of your conversations and can come
off looking like an idiot. Don't worry, this will not last long
and people will forget.

Saturday 21st

At last, the Sun moves into your sign. You will feel the heat now. You're chomping at the bit and have your Archer's bow and arrow ready to fire at your goals. Venus has moved into your last sector of dreams, solitude and secrets.

Sunday 22nd

Is it family time? Spend the day with your loved ones and share your enthusiasm. You will light up any family gathering from the minute they see you skipping down the path. This feels like the preparation for a race. The air is filled with anticipation around you. Let your arrow loose.

Monday 23rd

Your mood is still light-hearted and adventurous. You have a goal in mind. This is you at your best. Dreams seem more attainable. The worries that have followed you all year have dissolved. At least for now. Start the race while you can see the road ahead.

Tuesday 24th

Mercury is still in your psyche and today is telling Neptune what he has found. You already know what this is and this is why you're skipping. Enthusiasm fills you and you return to your creative projects. This influence may also mean that you have fallen in love.

Wednesday 25th

Mars is direct and still in his own sign. He has picked up speed since he turned and this is where your extra energy is coming from. You feel fired up and raring to go. Mercury's lead is already being turned into gold in the fire of your heart.

. . . .

Thursday 26th

The Moon meets with Mars today. This could be a very sexy day for you. Mars is happy and driven, the Moon is emotional and wants to connect. Mars also rules your sex drive. One warning though, don't be frivolous and overspend. This isn't something you want to be doing again.

Friday 27th

Venus in your dreams sector is quite the Siren. She may bewitch you easily. Please be sure that what you are looking at is the real thing and not a trick and don't rush into anything without careful research. There are other planetary connections which can rock you out of your happy boat now.

Saturday 28th

It's the weekend but you may need to come back down to Earth for a while. You must remember that life goes on while you are on cloud nine. There are duties that you must attend to now. This needs to be a busy Saturday of chores, so take the opportunity to get ahead now and make times for dreams later on.

Sunday 29th

Anything you feel rising from your subconscious will be felt in a big way today. Mercury is telling Jupiter what he has found and Jupiter tells the whole world. You might feel vulnerable and exposed. Take this lightly and laugh at yourself. Both Mercury and Jupiter like laughter.

Monday 30th

Today there is a Full Moon in your relationship sector. What have you been working towards for the last six months regarding partners? Under this illumination, you will be able to spot if anything new is going to last. It may be an illusion you have grasped onto with rose-tinted spectacles.

DECEMBER

. . . .

Tuesday 1st

Mercury moves into your sign. This heralds a busy time of communication and connecting. You will be researching all those places on your bucket list. New connections will be made with people who can help you go where you want to go. Your curiosity is alive and kicking now.

Wednesday 2nd

The Moon moves into your sex, death and rebirth sector. Unlike previous months when the Moon was here, you're now keen to explore secret and taboo subjects. You may be getting to know someone new on an intensely deep level. This is someone you can be vulnerable with.

Thursday 3rd

Whilst you are probing the depths of a new intimate relationship, you must ensure that you are not pushy and forceful. You might come across as being too demanding now. Be mindful of people's boundaries. Deepening connections must come from both parties. Mutual respect is always necessary.

Friday 4th

Today you may be thrilling someone with tales of your adventures and travel. You tell a good story but you must remember not to show-off. There's a chance that your enthusiasm and experience can overwhelm the listener. In which case, you will be seen as a know-it-all.

Saturday 5th

Your energy is back on track with your emotional life and a balance is found. However, the Moon is making a poor connection to Uranus in your health and duties sector. This means that you could be irritated that mundane activities take away some of your weekend time.

Sunday 6th

Dreamy, floaty energy comes from Venus in your hidden sector making a smooth connection to Neptune in your family sector. Venus mixes up a potion that makes this day surreal. You may be doing this to yourself with your escape mechanism of choice. Whatever your poison, play nicely and be careful.

Monday 7th

Monday comes and you settle back down into the working week. There could be a nice surprise waiting for you at work. You have great ideas and plans at this time. There's a chance that you find a solution to something that has been niggling you at work. Genius thinking is the energy of the day.

Tuesday 8th

Saturn is sitting in the very last degree of your money sector. This point is important and is a warning to consider all that you have learned here before he moves on. You'll have ten days to complete anything outstanding regarding finances, resources and the legacy you leave behind.

Wednesday 9th

The Moon moves into your social sector. A midweek evening with friends is possible. You could also be enjoying your friendship groups online. Chatty Mercury is joining the party and this is a great chance to connect with new people who share your interests. Don't stay up all night.

Thursday 10th

Females may charm you now. Watch for people who are trying to get you to do what they want. Don't let them convince you to do something you will regret. The Sun in your sign is connecting to Neptune and you could be fooled or the opposite, you could see false people for who they really are.

Friday 11th

The Sun joins a point in the sky where the past is brought back to your mind. Meanwhile, the Moon slips into your hidden sector of dreams. You will be reminiscing about someone or something from a long time ago. A deeply melancholic state comes over you. Regrets fill you.

Saturday 12th

The Moon is now sitting with Venus. Think of this like a Priestess and Sorceress discussing their art. Women will feature highly now. Mothers and other maternal figures, partners and lovers will all be floating around in your head. How have women in your life influenced you?

Sunday 13th

The Moon comes up from the underworld of your psyche and into the sector which deals with 'self'. This is a more accessible area and where you can deal with emotions easily. You can brush them off as they are more superficial now. Energy from the Sun in your sign is optimistic.

Monday 14th

There is an important New Moon, and this one sits on the point of looking to the past. It also joins Mercury who is contemplating life gone by too. You know that it's necessary to change something and make good intentions now. This is the perfect opportunity.

Tuesday 15th

Venus enters your sign now. She will bring her gifts of beauty, harmony, love and money. She also deals with self-worth. Here, she will end the year by making you take a hard look at how you handle money and responsibility. This is tied up with your self-worth.

Wednesday 16th

Saturn finally moves into your communications sector. You will be learning about how you can connect to the wider world. Friends far and wide will come under scrutiny for the next two and a half years. Some friends will be dropped. You may be antagonistic and raise a revolution now.

Thursday 17th

The Moon drifts by the planets that have been causing you trouble this year. She met Pluto yesterday and will fly by Jupiter and Saturn today. You give thanks for the hard lessons they have given you. This can make you feel proud and at the same time, very humble.

Friday 18th

Mercury is silent now. He's sitting in the light of the midwinter sun and receiving new information for the year ahead. A time of silent contemplation will be highly beneficial to you now. Go inside yourself, meditate and listen to your inner voice of calm.

Saturday 19th

Jupiter bids farewell to your money sector. Normally he would have expanded your finances but this year, combined with the other planets, he has expanded your debt. Nevertheless, you have managed to sort this out now. Don't overspend over the festive season and undo all your hard work.

Sunday 20th

A joyful union takes place in the heavens today. Jupiter and Saturn meet at the exact same degree in your communications sector. You will feel this as a push-pull energy but you must learn to ride it. Breathe in, breathe out. Speak, listen. Be active, be passive. This will help you to be an excellent communicator.

Monday 21st

The longest night, the Winter Solstice is here. The Sun is now in your money sector, this is good news. Mercury joins the Sun as his messenger. He is also the planet of merchants so you may want to consider buying and selling while he is in this sector.

Tuesday 22nd

After the stillness of the last few days, you ache for some action. Your creative sector is getting some Moon energy and you are drawn back to projects you are passionate about. You may show your divine essence now in all its glory. Make art to be proud of.

Wednesday 23rd

Your energy levels are revving up for the holidays. There may be some control issues, however. This influence may also mean that you need to watch your health as you are likely to overdo all the good things now. There may be some arguments between men and women.

Thursday 24th

The Moon dips into your health and duties sector. There's much work to do. If you are the one organising the activities for the holiday season then your mind will be focused on that. Alternatively, you could be the one being waited on and eating or drinking too much.

Friday 25th

Happy Christmas! The energy today is full of surprises. Fathers and sons can feature now as Jupiter and Saturn are still on the same degree. Conversations flow easily and it looks like Christmas will go well for you. Enjoy your day and the happy company you're with.

Saturday 26th

There's still nice, easy energy for the festive season. Family dreams and visions are mutual now. Everyone is happy and floats around in a Neptune sea of belonging and merging. There are jobs to be done today but these are shared and no-one feels over-worked.

Sunday 27th

The Moon moves into your relationship sector and you will concentrate more on your partner. The two of you can chat until the sun goes down. Conversations can go from the sublime to the ridiculous. There's a lot of laughter to be had if you let it.

Monday 28th

Today you may approach your partner with a vision of a brave new world. Don't be surprised if they don't buy it straight away. This is something that has been inside of you for a long time and they will need persuading that this can work for them too.

Tuesday 29th

The last Full Moon of the year falls in your sector of sex, death and rebirth. You may feel despondent now if you haven't had the courage to open up to someone close. If you were brave, then this Moon will highlight the good things that have come from that.

Wednesday 30th

The Moon opposite Mercury gives you the chance to review and assess how you deal with authority figures. Maternal and paternal figures who have formed your identity will enter your thoughts, you may even be considering your own nurturing and leadership roles. You must self-soothe and have a day free from family.

Thursday 31st

Today the energy suggests that there may be some issues that you cannot control. You must go with the flow now. A New Year's Eve at home with good food and company may be just the right recipe for a happy end to the year. Look back and give thanks.

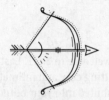

Sagittarius

DAILY FORECASTS
for 2021

JANUARY

. . . .

Friday 1st
Happy New Year and welcome to 2021. Last night's Full Moon may have seen you getting cosy and intimate with a lover. Today, the Moon has shifted into your outgoing travel sector and you are energised. You're raring to step into this year and have many plans.

Saturday 2nd
If there's something you need to say to a lover, say it soon. Mars is giving you the courage and strength to express yourself clearly now. You have extra energy to bring creative projects to completion. There's always a list of goals in your planner, finish some up before signing up for even more.

Sunday 3rd
You may already be in a productive frame of mind and eager to get back to work. The Moon is in your career sector and you're checking your planner and 'to do' lists. There may be a breakthrough with a problem that has puzzled you. Work and mundane duties fill your day.

Monday 4th
There's no need to make sacrifices today. Ensure that your work colleagues are not using you for their own gains. The Moon opposes Neptune and you ponder the difference between sacrifice and surrender. Just go with the flow but let no-one push you around or cross your personal boundaries.

Tuesday 5th

Your wider social groups help to balance what can be a
confusing day. Mercury meets Pluto in your finance and
value sector. You're being asked to make changes in how
you invest your time, money and energy. A money-making
scheme may come to light. Keep it to yourself for now.

Wednesday 6th

Mars is spending his final day in your creative sector.
Be loquacious and say what you mean. Send words of love
to someone special or make the first move. Start a creative
project now or decide which ones are no longer exciting you
and let them go.

Thursday 7th

As Mars jumps into your health and duties sector, you may
wish to join a gym or start a new fitness regime. Mars energy
will help you to stick at it now. Check in with your body and
ensure that you are getting your needs met. Watch where your
money goes today.

Friday 8th

A small crisis involving friends and money may arise. Don't
commit to anything that's out of your means right now. Check
all the facts and don't be seduced by possibilities. The Moon
shifts into your hidden sector where you will be detective-like
and do all your research.

Saturday 9th

Two planets shift signs. Venus leaves your own sign and enters your finance and value sector. You will get a better idea of what really means something to you now. Mercury flies into your communications sector and you may well raise a revolution while he's here.

Sunday 10th

Mercury bumps into Saturn. The teacher planet will observe how you communicate things you're passionate about. You must abide by the rules of etiquette and avoid gossip, untruths or hearsay. Continue with your mission of exposing injustices but be mindful of whose paths you may cross while doing so.

Monday 11th

Now Mercury visits Jupiter. You may find that you attract an audience for your speeches and this gives you more power. The downfall is that you may not see that your own ego is feeding on this and you become an obnoxious bore. Use this energy wisely and spread your words with respect.

Tuesday 12th

Mercury is squaring off with Uranus in your health and duties sector. Messages may turn into arguments or you may upset people you see every day. Pull yourself back a little and get a reality check. You're emotionally invested in making changes now.

Wednesday 13th

Today there's a New Moon in your finance and value sector. This is a great opportunity to make goals and intentions regarding money-making or seeing the real value in what you own. You may feel anxious and irritable today. Note what is triggering you and work it out at the gym.

Thursday 14th

The Sun meets Pluto. This may manifest as a battle of egos or control issues surrounding money and values. Meanwhile, the Moon is connecting with several planets making you unstable emotionally. You must lie low, say nothing and wait until this energy passes or you could be responsible for a conflict.

Friday 15th

There's gentle energy and you must use it to your benefit. An outgoing, altruistic Moon in your communications sector asks that you keep the peace and use your powers of speech to build bridges and not burn them. Share the love today, even if just on social media.

Saturday 16th

The peace continues as the Moon shifts into your family sector. A weekend with your nearest and dearest can help you to reconnect and find empathy and compassion for others. You can be idealistic now, but this will not hurt. This is a nice day for reminiscing.

Sunday 17th

The Moon meets Neptune. This has the effect of blinding you to reality momentarily. Neptune's dream-like qualities can whisk you away to a fantasy land where everything is rosy. Keep one foot on the ground, you still have mundane jobs to do today. Try sharing responsibilities with other family members.

Monday 18th

Jupiter and Uranus are squaring off today. Any unrest in conversations or your duties will feel larger than it is. You may get a minor health niggle. You have much to say and do but don't know where to start. Pick one task only and go from there.

Tuesday 19th

The Sun enters your communications sector. You will now be a force to be reckoned with. People will listen to what you have to say. If a revolution is what you want, make sure you're doing it for the right reasons. You're passionate, persuasive and charismatic.

Wednesday 20th

Mars and Uranus meet up. This can be highly volatile energy and made bigger by a connection to Jupiter who expands everything. A health problem may come to a head and need attention. Be careful out there on the roads as road rage is very likely. Lie low today.

Thursday 21st

The Moon meets the troublesome twosome, Mars and Uranus.
You may be drawn into unnecessary dramas and find it difficult
to emotionally detach. Get all your duties done and then go
and hide. This energy can be draining so stay home and treat
yourself with comfort foods or favourite books.

Friday 22nd

Today you may feel more in control but need more time than
usual to process your thoughts. You will be thinking before you
speak your mind. Venus helps you to put yourself first today and
Pluto hints that there are things or people you need to release
from your life.

Saturday 23rd

The Moon shifts into your relationship sector this morning.
You take joy in speaking fervently to a close business or love
partner. Venus and Neptune connect to allow you a dreamy time.
You may think about a home make-over and this excites you.
Mars' tension still lingers so be careful today.

Sunday 24th

The Sun meets Saturn in your communication sector. This can
be difficult as Saturn likes to quash any egotistical notions you
may have. However, if you show yourself authentically, Saturn
can be your best guide. Chatty times with a lover make you
happy and you talk into the small hours.

Monday 25th

Mars and Jupiter are still at war. You will find that there's a strong likelihood of your intentions being misunderstood. You may also be over-assertive and slightly aggressive. Check in with yourself before pointing the finger and blaming someone else for the tension in the air.

Tuesday 26th

The Moon is now in your intimacy sector and you desire to hide away with someone special. You may be over-protective of another or you may be feeling vulnerable yourself. Listen to your intuition now and it will tell you how best to nurture and comfort yourself and those close to you.

Wednesday 27th

Today you find it difficult to see any value in your immediate environment. You may yearn to get away and be looked after by another, but this is self-avoidance. This is just a passing Moon phase, but it triggers you into thinking about what you need and what you want.

Thursday 28th

A Full Moon in your travel sector brings out the explorer in you. Perhaps you're more at home in strange places. Perhaps you need to conquer somewhere before calling it home. Difficult connections to the Moon make you tricky to deal with today. You are pushy and obnoxious.

Friday 29th

The Sun meets Jupiter and you must take advantage of this
highly beneficial energy in your communications sector. If you
want a raise, ask for it now. If you have something to say, go
ahead. Just be mindful not to let your ego lead. Let people see
the authentic you.

Saturday 30th

Use today to prepare for Mercury's first retrograde of the year.
Back up all your devices and double-check travel plans. Take extra
care with things and don't commit to signing legal documents
just yet. Your communications sector will be affected so practice
pausing before responding.

Sunday 31st

Mercury retrograde begins. Take everything slowly now.
The Moon in your career sector gets you into efficiency
mode so you're already checking the calendar and making
sure nothing is double-booked. You've no time for the
frivolous fantasies Neptune is offering you, keep your mind
focused and clear today.

FEBRUARY

....

Monday 1st

Venus glides into your communications sector. She'll help to
soften any blows from the Mercury retrograde. You may find
that you're extra patient, compassionate and mindful when
speaking and listening now. Mars and Sun are squaring off,
watch that you don't get exhausted.

Tuesday 2nd

The Moon is in your social sector. You're emotionally pulled
to achieving harmony within your wider groups. You may be
called to act as a mediator at these times. Nice connections to
the Sun and Jupiter rain blessings on your social interactions.
You have plenty of support from your friends.

Wednesday 3rd

This afternoon the Moon dips down into your hidden sector
where you can be super-secretive and enjoy the sense of an
alter-ego. Your darker parts live here, and you fear exposure,
yet you enjoy what you learn here. Mars and Venus aren't
talking, expect to see lovers' tiffs.

Thursday 4th

A difficult Moon sits opposite Mars and Uranus. This has the effect
of stirring up something from your psyche. It'll be uncomfortable
but is the start of a healing process. Shadow material surfaces
and gives you something to contemplate. You will enjoy this deep
journey of self-discovery.

Friday 5th

Stay with the unconscious material making itself known.
Pluto is connecting to help make the necessary transformation
of something dark and ugly into a priceless treasure. This is
important work. You may not be able to think it through clearly
just yet, wait until the Mercury retrograde is over.

Saturday 6th

Venus meets Saturn in your communication sector. You may
find that you come up against a teacher or elder who puts
you straight on a few things. This is accepted easily as you
have total respect for the person who fills this role. What will
you learn?

Sunday 7th

The Moon crosses the point of past karma and there's a sense
that you leave something behind. This may be tiny, but you feel
it. You may have a moment of panic or grief due to Neptune
connecting and wanting everything to feel nice. This is baggage
you no longer need.

Monday 8th

Mercury is in the heart of the Sun. It's your job to listen out
for messages. Pay attention to dreams and symbols and note
anything significant. You may feel irritable and not know why.
Check your jobs list, there may be something outstanding that
needs a last-minute boost.

Tuesday 9th

The Moon connects to very different energies today. From your sector of finances and value, you'll feel assertive, then unrealistic before you fix on what you have to do. Finances shared with another may be out of date or subscriptions need renewing. Scrutinise your bank balance and look for these.

Wednesday 10th

This is an emotionally challenging day as the Moon meets the planets in your communications sector. You may have big ideas to discuss but feel restricted, irritable and undervalued. Don't hold back, you have ideas worth sharing and people need to hear them. Be bold and brave.

Thursday 11th

Today there's a New Moon in your communications sector. Be careful what you wish for as this is connected to Mercury retrograde. Make an intention to revisit, redo or revise an existing topic of research. Venus and Jupiter combine to give you as much luck as you deserve.

Friday 12th

As the Moon enters your family sector, it's possible that you feel the shift. You may become more insular and wish to enjoy family time at home. Your loved ones can be lively or loving but together you may come up with new ideas or new ways of doing ordinary jobs.

Saturday 13th

Neptune gets a visit from the Moon today. You'll feel nostalgic and reminisce about memorable family times. Mercury retrograde meets Venus and this can throw a spanner in the works when talking to a lover. Be mindful that your words may be misunderstood. Be as clear as you can.

Sunday 14th

Mercury backs into Jupiter. Any retrograde effect will be made much larger. As Jupiter is your ruler, you may be lucky, but he may also expose a lie or hurtful gossip. Be prepared to back up what you say when called upon. Don't get involved.

Monday 15th

You're inspired and goal orientated. Saturn and Jupiter help to ensure that your duties and responsibilities are all done with ease and satisfaction. A connection to Mercury retrograde may make you overly-direct and forceful when communicating but this can be part of what makes your day productive.

Tuesday 16th

Go through your checklist, as there's something there that requires your attention. You're climbing a small mountain and may have skipped a few important steps. Go back and check as this will become evident later on if not rectified now. Your words are accepted with grace and love today.

. . . .

Wednesday 17th

The Moon enters your health and duties sector. Connections from Uranus and Saturn mean that you may come across a stumbling block or experience some illness. Have you overdone it? It's likely that you have unwittingly upset an elder or person in authority and caused some friction.

Thursday 18th

The Sun enters your family sector bringing light and warmth to your tribe. This is a fun time to merge and connect with your nearest and dearest. Organise family vacations or day trips now. Your heart and energy are in sync. Do what you love and love what you do.

Friday 19th

Venus and Mars aren't friends today. The celestial lovers aren't connecting. You may see trouble brewing between men and women in your communications and duties sectors. You'll be unable to please everyone today so don't exhaust yourself trying. Choose your battles, some aren't worth your energy.

Saturday 20th

The Moon is in your relationships sector. Spending time with a lover will leave you feeling hoarse. You two can talk and talk. Solving problems or discussing weird and wonderful concepts is what keeps your most important relationships alive. Mercury loves to see and hear this.

Sunday 21st

Mercury turns direct. Feel free to sign that contract or get a haircut. The Moon meets the point of fate in Mercury's sign and you may feel compelled to make plans to study a course of higher education. Venus has a say in this, she loves the idea and supports you.

Monday 22nd

This morning the Moon shifts and you begin the week in a reserved mood. You wish to feel nurtured and safe and observe those around you from the safety of your home. Someone, a lover perhaps, may be trying to get you out of your comfort zone.

Tuesday 23rd

The cautious Moon connects to dreamy Neptune. You may be drifting off to faraway places in your mind. You're yearning for something that you cannot quite put your finger on. This may be a concept you wish to learn more about or a person you would like to know better.

Wednesday 24th

The Moon opposes Pluto and you don't feel in control. Your instinct is to pull back and retreat until you feel safe again. Mars is giving you courage but if you need to be invisible, simply have a quiet day and listen to what your intuition says.

Thursday 25th

The Moon has shifted, and your bravery has returned. A fire sign like you needs to burn and glow with passion. You face much opposition today, but you deal with it fairly. There's the possibility of a tantrum but as Venus is entering your family sector, it will not be from there.

Friday 26th

Today has a strange mix of outright bravery and authenticity mingled with ethereal, unrealistic dreams. The Moon opposes Venus and they vie for top feminine position. See if you can combine this energy and have the courage to make a dream come true. Go after what you want.

Saturday 27th

A Full Moon in your career sector will illuminate all your achievements over the last six months. What you have worked hard for will now reap rewards. You may be too modest and shy away from attention. Stand up, take the credit, it's yours and you deserve it.

Sunday 28th

There's a lot of earth energy around. Use it wisely and do some grounding exercises. Take a walk in nature, do yoga, cook, eat, have sex or do some gardening. Your natural fire needs fuel to burn so do something that excites you and follow your passion.

MARCH

· · · · · · · · · · · · · · · · ·

Monday 1st

Your social groups are in the spotlight today. The planets in
your communication sector allow you to speak freely with
respect for others. An interest may be widened, or you may
investigate a deep subject now. Joining like-minded groups will
be a great advantage to your never-ending search for truth.

Tuesday 2nd

When the Moon drops into your hidden sector, you have time
to ruminate and think about what has piqued your interest
recently. This could be something that may be frowned upon
by normal society. You may be looking at the arts of alchemy,
astrology and healing now.

Wednesday 3rd

You're not easily shocked but remember that others are.
Keep your mysterious thoughts to yourself for now.
Venus and the Sun in your family sector show that you're
naturally inclined to be the one who delves into the taboo
and your family understand, even if they have no interest
themselves.

Thursday 4th

Be careful that you haven't stepped onto a path that you
cannot deal with. You may be having second thoughts as your
rational mind is sending you messages. Neptune, however, is
quite happy to support you on an adventure into the unknown.
Stay safe and take one step at a time.

Friday 5th

The Moon enters your sign. It immediately opposes Mars making you slightly aggressive and self-righteous with a lover or another important person. Mercury meets Jupiter again and this enhances any speech-making or philosophising you do today. Be careful as this combination can make you an egotistical bore.

Saturday 6th

The Moon now connects to Jupiter and Mercury. You're filled with your own self-projection. Be careful who you are mouthing off to as you may pick someone who will give you a taste of your own medicine. Alternatively, you may find a sympathetic audience who allow you to vent.

Sunday 7th

Today you're brought back to your mundane duties and Sunday chores. This is fine as you're happy to be helpful. You have a spring in your step and find new ways of doing otherwise boring things. There's time at the end of the day to self-indulge.

Monday 8th

The Moon in your finance and values sector connects to Neptune. You may start to see things around you in a new light. A different perspective helps to make sure that you're aligned with your true north and Neptune is your compass here. Use self-discipline and avoid unrealistic goals.

Tuesday 9th

Pluto says hello to the Moon now and has something to say about your recent thoughts. What needs to be transformed or released from your life? Clear the way by decluttering material objects which have no real use or value to you. Talk this over with a close friend or lover.

Wednesday 10th

The Sun meets Neptune in your family sector. Neptune's mists are burned away, and you may start seeing something or someone in their true light. As the Moon passes Saturn and Jupiter, you find yourself being judgemental; stay compassionate and respectful to those who differ greatly from you.

Thursday 11th

In your communication sector, the Moon meets Mercury. Your heart and mind have a talk. It's possible that you reprimand yourself for excluding someone recently. The Moon shifts into your compassionate family sector later and you reach out to merge with those who you call your tribe.

Friday 12th

Today there's relatively easy energy and the weekend begins on a serene note. Uranus connects nicely, and this unpredictable energy can bring surprises or revelations. Romantic feelings combined with the electric charge from Uranus can produce poetry or art. With family involved, expect a fun day of connection.

Saturday 13th

A beautiful New Moon in your family sector gives you a great opportunity to set goals and intentions. Think about how you may have had some idea of your true north. Neptune sits with this Moon to remind and guide you. Pluto is in the wings waiting to help you transform.

Sunday 14th

Today the mood shifts and you're more outgoing. You have many plans in your mind and need to get something down on paper. Make lists, check your schedules and bank balance. Venus meets Neptune and confirms that what you do now is essential for you to blossom and grow.

Monday 15th

Jupiter now adds his opinion to your plans. He makes your ideas and intentions even bigger. Don't let this get out of hand, keep it simple and attainable and keep it true. Your inner work will be hard, don't overload yourself with unrealistic targets.

Tuesday 16th

Your ego may get the better of you today. The Sun connects to Pluto and you may already be de-cluttering like a maniac. However, the Moon squaring off with Pluto triggers you and you may feel regret or guilt. Pull back a little, this Moon phase will pass quickly enough.

Wednesday 17th

It's possible that you feel extra irritable or restless. This is the Moon sitting with edgy Uranus in your health and duties sector. Do all your mundane chores and check in with your health. Recent high activity may have caused adrenaline levels to rise and now they have dropped again.

Thursday 18th

Make time today for self-care. Be indulgent and take a bubble bath or cook your favourite meal. Neptune and Venus will support this. You don't have to be the 'go-to' person all the time. Let people know when you need a break and learn to say 'No' sometimes.

Friday 19th

The Moon has moved into your relationship sector and met Mars. Emotional energy will be high and maybe even sexy. You don't need to talk today as Mercury is at odds with the Moon so find other ways to connect to someone special. Keep a low fire burning.

Saturday 20th

Today is the Spring Equinox. Day and night are equal lengths. This is a great time to pause and reflect on the year so far. Where do you see yourself exploring as the longer days approach? Your ruler, Jupiter, is connecting and asks how far you're willing to spread your wings.

Sunday 21st

With the Sun now heating up your creative sector, you may see a new romance or artistic project to excite you. Venus also enters this sector to harmonise and beautify what you do here. Mercury and Uranus connect, and you spontaneously share your dreams with someone close.

Monday 22nd

Give your lover a chance to get to know you on a deeper level. The Moon is in your intimacy sector where topics such as sex, death and rebirth are explored. You're already becoming open to these things. Mercury connects to make you articulate how you feel about these things.

Tuesday 23rd

The Moon opposes Pluto. Your safety and comfort zones may feel threatened. Maybe this trigger is to show you where intimacy truly lies. Pluto asks for death and rebirth. Something in you is changing. Are you aware of what that is? Neptune is your inner compass, follow your dreams.

Wednesday 24th

Venus is in the heart of the Sun in your creative sector. This can be a time of romance or self-care. A helpful connection from the Moon means that you're emotionally invested in feeling good today. Your rational mind will have other ideas and cause you some inner conflict.

Thursday 25th

A fiery Moon in your travel sector takes you exploring new cultures and lands in order to align yourself with your true north. You will have much to think about now. Higher education may be a great opportunity to do some research. Mercury, your mind, is undecided at the moment.

Friday 26th

Today your emotional self has a more rational outlook.
You're checking all the details and ensuring that you have
the facts. Recent interests still need to have a logical basis
for you otherwise you may discard them. You are more
grounded and determined to make solid plans.

Saturday 27th

You're emotionally drained as the Moon opposes Mercury and
Neptune. It's difficult for you to fix on one train of thought.
Being angry or irritable with yourself will not help. Take time
to pause and consider all options. Don't let the moment cloud
your judgement.

Sunday 28th

A Full Moon in your social sector will show you who your
friends and allies are. You'll have a keen sense of discernment
and will be able to cut people out of your life. Make sure that
you do this with love and compassion. Know that they simply
do not align with you.

Monday 29th

Assertiveness can be your friend or foe. The Moon in your
social sector connects to both Mars and Jupiter. Aggression can
get out of hand when Jupiter is involved. If you use this energy
wisely, you'll be able to stay focused on tasks and achieve a lot.

Tuesday 30th

Keep one foot on the ground. Your mind will be so full of chatter you may be tempted to switch off and enter a fantasy world instead. The Moon makes awkward connections to several planets and you may see control issues and power struggles going on.

Wednesday 31st

If you did disengage with real life yesterday, you've entered your mind space which can be dark and mysterious. You're quite happy here with the Moon connecting to Mercury and Neptune. Wander around your psyche and look for clues to guide you home to your authentic self.

APRIL

. . . .

Thursday 1st

The Moon lands in your sign this morning. You're outgoing
and ready for action. Any changes you feel need to be made
have a good chance of being done so without too much stress.
This can include a make-over at home or a new hairstyle.

Friday 2nd

Mercury spends his final days in your family sector. He connects
to Pluto now and asks for his new mission before he enters the
first sign. Listen carefully to cues and triggers to show you
the way. This may be an emotionally draining day so preserve
your energy for activities that nourish you.

Saturday 3rd

Your heart and mind have another talk today. The Moon in
your sign is resistant to the changes Pluto asks for. Mercury
needs you to use your rational mind and stay logical. This will
be easier this evening when the Moon shifts to your hard-
working finances and value sector.

Sunday 4th

Mercury has now settled into your creative sector. You have
many plans, but you must sort through them and decide
which ones are really worth your efforts. Venus is your
warrior Goddess in this sector, and she will support any
decision as long as it doesn't diminish you.

Monday 5th

The Moon meets Pluto. What you do now, can feel like a crisis or betrayal to parts of yourself. Know that there can be no growth without change and Pluto is asking you to reveal the gold hidden inside you. Your heart and mind align in the afternoon and you're ready.

Tuesday 6th

Communication is the key. You may learn something from an elder or a person in authority. Listen carefully as this will be good advice. Venus and Mars help to make a love connection sweet. You can brainstorm and come up with new exciting ways of doing old, boring things.

Wednesday 7th

You meet another influential person. Jupiter acts as the truth or the law and when he meets the Moon, you feel your heart surge. This is a cue to show you're on the right track. Great connections to Venus and Mars keep the love train rolling.

Thursday 8th

A dreamy Moon in your family sector takes you on a journey which stirs up long-forgotten emotions. This is a pleasant experience as Uranus the disruptor is involved. You may reconnect with a long-lost friend or get an 'aha!' moment about a conundrum that has been bothering you.

Friday 9th

Neptune hosts the Moon. Pause, reflect and get some perspective on where you're going. Acceptance and surrender may be your only ways forward. Mars tells you that this can be tough on your mental faculties but stick with it and you'll be victorious. What you need to conquer is yourself.

Saturday 10th

The Moon picks up the pace when it moves into your creative sector. Mercury and Saturn help you to think clearly and responsibly. Venus and Jupiter give you the go-ahead with their many blessings. This is your chance to shine and show the world what you're made of.

Sunday 11th

Your head and heart are as aligned as they can possibly be. The Moon meets Mercury and although your mind is busy with new ideas, plans and concepts, your heart takes it all in. You're falling in love with the new you, who is about to rise.

Monday 12th

A New Moon in your creative sector is your green light. Take control and lay the foundations now. Set up a vision board and express yourself honestly. This may feel strange and you experience some resistance but once you start you will not look back. Plant those seeds now.

Tuesday 13th

Your health and duties sector needs your attention now. You may feel anxious and ready to fly before you can walk. Hold back and remember that you are only in the beginning stages of a new growth cycle. Self-care is paramount now. Check in with your body's needs.

Wednesday 14th

Venus spends her last day in your creative sector. If you have words of love, express them. If you have a burning need to add beauty somewhere, do it. Splash some colour around and brighten up a dull spot. Find that neglected project and give it one last push.

Thursday 15th

This morning your love life calls and time with a special person becomes necessary. You need to talk and talk. Mars and Jupiter combine to give you huge amounts of energy and optimism. Venus quietly steps into your health and duties sector to remind you to take care of your body.

Friday 16th

You may come to a standstill today. Fear not, this is simply a chance for you to peek over the horizon and make an agenda. The point of fate meets the Moon and you feel the pull. Is this your inner compass calling? Stay positive and take some rest.

Saturday 17th

Mercury is very busy making many connections. In your health and duties sector, his job is to make connections that serve you. This is a two-way thing and you'll also see how you can serve others. Mercury loves commerce so use the barter system now. Exchange ideas with others.

Sunday 18th

Nourish yourself with what feeds your soul. This may be those topics you only think about when alone. Today is a day of rest as Mercury is silent, however, Venus and Uranus demand that you soothe yourself. Meditation or gardening may help. Get in touch with your body now.

Monday 19th

Mercury and the Sun jump into your health and duties sector together. This is a time of high activity where you may see yourself as a guiding light for others. Good for you, this will not only give them courage and hope but will also support your own endeavours.

Tuesday 20th

There's a lot of fixed energy and this may make you feel stuck. If you're unsure of how to move next, stay still, this feeling will soon pass. Ignore the little voice inside you which says you are being foolish. You're a brave explorer, and you can find new frontiers.

Wednesday 21st

Your inner critic is trying to make you pause in your proceedings. This makes you edgy and restless. Use that electric energy and produce something. Saturn is concerned you may be stretching yourself too far so understand your limits and abide by them until you are surer of your convictions.

Thursday 22nd

Today you're a force to be reckoned with. The Moon is in your career sector and gives you the drive to succeed and be seen doing so. This is a day for showing what you are made of. If you have a presentation to make, you will be victorious.

Friday 23rd

Venus meets Uranus. You could be in for a surprise from a loved one. You're hard-working and deserve a treat, watch what comes your way. You're beaming with light that others will want a part of, make sure they don't diminish yours.

Saturday 24th

You have no time for dreams and fantasies today. Keep it real and don't get drawn into Neptune's waters. The Moon invites you to enjoy time with your wider social groups but beware. Mercury and Uranus have met, this is blabbermouth energy. Watch what you say, don't betray a confidence.

Sunday 25th

Mercury now meets Venus and they share some words on looking after your own needs. They are both squaring off with Saturn so you must be sure not to be selfish or cross personal boundaries. An outgoing friendly Moon just wants you to have fun with friends today.

Monday 26th

You're optimistic and energetic. However, you're ready for some alone time in the evening to recharge your batteries. You can delight in your own company and your weird and wonderful ways of entertaining yourself. Your deepest, darkest parts enjoy the monthly visit to your psyche and its workings.

Tuesday 27th

A Full Moon in your hidden sector acts like a light bulb and shows you all the pieces of you that need healing. You're not afraid of this. The Moon opposes Venus, Mercury and Uranus but this serves to make you determined to find the gold in your shadow.

Wednesday 28th

Pluto, the planet of transformation and permanent change, goes retrograde today. Here's where the hard work starts. As he is sitting in your finance and value sector this will be time for a massive clear out. Take a hard look at your home, your bank balance and your value system.

Thursday 29th

The Moon has returned to your sign. This can make you
optimistic and outgoing but can also make you a headstrong
bore. Saturn is connecting so ensure that it's not the latter
that the teacher planet sees, or you will be given detention and
extra homework.

Friday 30th

If you're feeling super-charged and full of restless energy,
blame the Sun and Uranus. This annual combination can
be the trigger for genius and innovative ways of thinking or
dealing with issues in your health and duties sector. You may
even get a headache as a result.

MAY

. . . .

Saturday 1st

There's still a huge amount of energy for you to harness and use to your benefit. On a simple level, you may get all your chores done with time to spare and enjoy the weekend. If you're prone to burning out, take things easy, as you may not realise you when you have overdone things.

Sunday 2nd

Venus and Mercury are spending their last week in your health and duties sector. This is a good time to schedule all the health checks you may need. It could also be a time to take a break, catch up with friends and do things that make you feel good.

Monday 3rd

The Moon meets Saturn in your communications sector. You may find that you seek the advice of an elder or boss. Venus and Neptune are making a great connection and you may enjoy a romantic or self-indulgent time. Dream big and make intentions for yourself now.

Tuesday 4th

Mercury flies into your relationship sector. Expect the next few weeks to be very busy with endless chatter with your lover. Swapping ideas with a special person may broaden your horizons and set you on a course of study. You'll be thinking aloud now so watch what you say.

Wednesday 5th

Jupiter, your ruler, greets the Moon. Emotions may be unusually high. This afternoon, as the Moon shifts, you may feel pulled in different directions. Your energy and emotions may not be in sync. Take this time to pause before proceeding with any definite course of action.

Thursday 6th

The Moon in your dreamy, family sector makes you romantic and idealistic. You may be reminiscing about your childhood and wondering where your childhood dreams are now. Did you manage to achieve any? Is there something you need to get off your chest today? Jupiter urges you speak out now.

Friday 7th

As you get ready for the weekend, your creative side appears and gives you all sorts of ideas to work with. There may be a project you've neglected which you look at with new eyes. A second chance to give something a make-over, including yourself, is there for you to grab.

Saturday 8th

You may have trouble with expressing your own needs. Be careful that others don't try to manage your weekend for you. This may cause some grief and conflict. Words are better than action today as Mercury knows. You may need to ask for a second opinion from someone wise.

Sunday 9th

Venus now enters your relationship sector. The planet of love can only be a good thing here. This is a great day to celebrate the little luxuries of life such as good food and great company. The Moon in Venus' sign enhances the need to add beauty and harmony to your day.

Monday 10th

The Moon makes her monthly visit to Uranus in your health and duties sector. As Mars is connecting here too, you may be run off your feet with tasks. You have energy, but this may be in short, sharp bursts. It's possible that you wear yourself out.

Tuesday 11th

A New Moon in your health and duties sector is the excuse you need to assess your mundane jobs and make changes. If you have too much that's weighing you down, now is the time to let some go. Quality is more important than quantity.

Wednesday 12th

The Moon meets Venus in your relationship sector. Aim for a midweek date with your lover. Between the two of you, you put the world to rights and exchange interesting concepts. You can overcome many obstacles by sharing a problem with someone special today. Two heads are better than one.

Thursday 13th

You're really speaking from the heart today. The Moon meets Mercury and you say what you mean and more. It's possible that your family recognise that you need a break from mundane duties, and you may be released from some. Remember not to sacrifice yourself for others.

Friday 14th

Jupiter dips into your family sector. This will be like having an elder or authority figure step in and try to take control. Jupiter wants to bring joy, luck and optimism. You may see a benefactor or figure from the law come to help out with family business. Be open-minded.

Saturday 15th

This is a quiet day where you may have much to think about. Your home and heart need attention and you find that this weekend will be mostly spent with family. Is there something that threatens your security or your family unit? You're feeling extra protective of your kin.

Sunday 16th

As the Moon meets Mars today it's possible that you're emotionally invested in something that triggers you into action. Something may anger you and make you quick to fly into a temper. This actually may be the only way to rouse others and sort a problem out together.

Monday 17th

Your mood may be quick-tempered and fiery today. You're looking for answers and may be pushy and brutal. You will need to curb the impulse to be self-righteous and grandiose. Use your leadership skills to probe but do it with compassion and respect at all times.

Tuesday 18th

As the Moon opposes Saturn you may come up against a stumbling block. You have maybe gone too far and broken through someone's personal boundaries. Time to pull back, apologise and learn to be more respectful in future. This is easier said than done but will be a valuable lesson for you.

Wednesday 19th

Your recent fiery mood starts to calm down. You may hear some information that you take on board. The Moon's opposition to Jupiter can feel like a tumble with the legal system. Accept that you're not always in the right and take the ticking off you receive.

Thursday 20th

The Moon in your career sector gives you the rational mind you have lacked in recent days. You may have to pause and reflect before taking further action. You will be commended for the passion you have for certain projects and your fiery insistence to see justice done.

Friday 21st

The Sun sits in your relationship sector. Enjoy a month of light, warmth and illumination with your lover. You begin by making sure that you have all the facts and that everything is in order. You may find yourself decluttering or taking a detox from the recent tension.

Saturday 22nd

The Moon dips into your social sector. It's time to unwind from a stressful week and have fun with friends. You may enjoy this on a superficial level only. If you try to speak about your dreams and creative concepts, it will fall on deaf ears.

Sunday 23rd

Saturn turns retrograde today. What follows will be a few months of having to take a serious look at how you communicate. Your style may need to change, or you may have a new perspective and abandon interest groups you have been involved with. Some friendships may need to be lovingly released.

Monday 24th

You may be having a moment of conscience right now. You feel that you should be acting on something dear to you, but your wisdom tells you to hang back. Restless energy takes you to your deeply intense thoughts. Process these while the Moon is in your hidden sector.

Tuesday 25th

Today you may feel obstructed and blocked. This is Saturn, newly retrograde, asking you to be aware of personal boundaries. You may have the energy and vision to march an army across the country but there are borders you have to observe and respect. Feel your way in patiently.

Wednesday 26th

A Full Moon drops into your sign. This is a huge spotlight on your emotions and will show up any successes and growth from the last six months. What has come to completion? What are you thankful for? Have you learned from any mistakes?

Thursday 27th

Today you may feel like a failure. Don't take this to heart as this is just a passing Moon phase making difficult connections to Venus and Mercury in your relationship sector. Listen to your inner voice and find validation there, not in other people. Be gentle with yourself.

Friday 28th

You shake out of your low mood and have more optimism now. Mercury goes retrograde tomorrow so use today to make all the necessary preparations and back up all your devices. You need distraction today and this will suit you. Stay busy and technical and ensure you've not missed anything.

Saturday 29th

Venus meets Mercury as he goes retrograde. This will occur through your relationship sector. Keep things low key and respectful. Communications can get lost or be misunderstood now so do things the old-fashioned way and speak face to face to ensure clarity on all sides.

Sunday 30th

The energy today is gentle and flowing. You may wish to connect with others and back a good cause. This kind of thing will make you feel a good citizen of the world. A local event may get your attention. Get involved, you have what it takes to rally the troops.

Monday 31st

The Moon meets newly retrograde Saturn. You sit up and listen to good advice rather than stubbornly refuse to co-operate. Mercury also connects to the Moon, this is a day where you are tested. Put your energy into what feeds your soul and stay out of things which don't concern you.

JUNE

....

Tuesday 1st

You may be extra sensitive to the plights of family members today. Remember that Jupiter expands everything he touches and today he contacts the Moon, your emotions. You may be pulled towards a future vision as the Sun meets the point of fate. What can you see ahead?

Wednesday 2nd

Venus is about to leave your relationship sector. You should use this critical energy to reassure a lover and express how you feel. Mercury may be hard on you, but Venus will aim to deepen the connection you share now. A midweek date night could be just what you need.

Thursday 3rd

It's likely that you'll want to have time alone. Your patience may be tested regarding relationships and you'll need to process this in your own time. Neptune meets the Moon and asks that you allow fantasy thinking only if it's in alignment with your desires.

Friday 4th

Today you're full of potential. Your busy mind is already devising new plans and creating ambitious projects. Have you had an idea of where your near future lies? You have a lot of energy and optimism now, just be sure not to burn out too quickly.

Saturday 5th

Mars and Pluto are in opposition. This can be tough as you find that you may not be in control of a situation. The Moon squares off with both and you're disheartened. Don't give up, this is a brief period of interruption. Remember to breathe and release.

Sunday 6th

Jupiter helps you out of a low mood and gives you the get up and go you need to get all chores done. Venus reminds you to protect your own energy as you plod steadily through your task list. Go slowly today and do everything with focused determination.

Monday 7th

You may feel restless when the Moon meets Uranus but there's a good side to this energy. It may be a niggle telling you to go even slower. It may also be the jolt that reminds you of a detail you might have forgotten. Do everything by the rules today.

Tuesday 8th

Something small but very important needs your attention. Pluto is asking you to check your bank balance. Mars is also sitting in a sector relating to money so perhaps it's a good idea to go through your finances and see what has been overlooked or out of date.

Wednesday 9th

You're drawn to spend time with a lover and test the waters. There's a deep desire to know if you're on the same page and headed towards a future together. Mercury retrograde in this sector isn't the best time to do this, but you should think about it.

Thursday 10th

A New Moon meets Mercury retrograde. Your thoughts and emotions may be muddled, and you cannot get clarity. Know that this phase will pass quickly but make intentions to investigate when the energy is better. You may get into deep water if you persist at this time.

Friday 11th

Mercury has nothing to say to you today. He's in the heart of the Sun, listening. You must do the same. Be aware of any messages such as gossip, coincidences or dream symbols. Mars marches into your fiery travel sector. It is time to plan your summer holidays or new studies.

Saturday 12th

The Moon meets Venus. You may feel like curling up in a ball and eating your favourite ice cream under a blanket. This energy calls for you to protect yourself and those you love. Comforting meals which remind you of childhood may be on the menu. You reminisce with mothers and daughters.

Sunday 13th

You're especially protective of your own needs today. The Moon opposes Pluto, and this can feel threatening and controlling. When the Moon shifts and meets Mars, you're on the defensive and ready to fight for those you love. Evaluate the battlefield first, the threat may be imagined.

Monday 14th

This is a difficult day and you may feel like a small child being reprimanded. A fiery Moon opposes Saturn, who is very strict on you. Tears may well up, or worse, you may have a tantrum. Lie low if you can and avoid anyone with a big ego.

Tuesday 15th

The tension continues and you may just blow like a volcano.
Remember that Mercury is causing some upset in your
relationship sector. It's possible that you're blowing your own
trumpet and coming across as pushy and obnoxious. Be mindful
how you communicate with important people now.

Wednesday 16th

This morning your logical mind brings you back to your
centre. You will need to reflect on your recent behaviour
and evaluate how that has made you appear. Pay attention to
detail today at work. Be methodical and declutter your work
environment. This will help bring you a calmer mind.

Thursday 17th

You have no time for fancies or idealistic thinking today.
You're goal-orientated, and desire to achieve more harmony.
Mercury may give you the slip today as you leave no stone
unturned and ensure that you have all the facts in front of you.
You may surprise a few people.

Friday 18th

This morning your mind turns towards the weekend and how
you might spend it with your social groups. Think of those
who energise you and make plans with them. Your social
media contacts are included here. Lovingly leave those groups
which antagonise you and leave you feeling disempowered.

Saturday 19th

You may just have to go along with the majority today if you're
going out with friends. It may not be quite your thing that's
planned but go anyway. You may find that you learn something
or touch on a subject that is new and different to you.

Sunday 20th

The Moon drops into your hidden sector where you may
be digging up your own dirt and self-analysing. Your secret
thoughts and inner workings will shock some people which is
why you tend to keep them to yourself until ready for exposure.
Spend some time alone today and try not to shock yourself.

Monday 21st

Today is the Summer Solstice. The longest day of the year
brings Jupiter retrograde with it. This will also have you
looking at how you communicate, but especially with the
law. Your quest for truth ad wisdom may go in a different
direction. Stay open-minded and listen more than talk.

Tuesday 22nd

Mercury turns direct today. This is good news. You will get more
clarity now about how your relationships are evolving. You may
revisit your thoughts of a shared future and re-envision those
goals. Venus and Neptune support this endeavour and bless your
efforts to merge with and love another.

Wednesday 23rd

Your mind and heart may not be in sync today, but this will
pass quickly. You feel an emotional pull towards the past and
you may grieve over something you've had to let go. Venus and
Pluto are opposing each other, expect to see control or power
struggles.

Thursday 24th

A Full Moon in your finances and value sector illuminates what you feel is important to you. Self-worth is also included here. Look around you and see what brings you joy and what does not. You can be too strict on yourself sometimes, allow a little luxury in.

Friday 25th

Neptune, the planet of mystery and illusion goes retrograde today. This can herald a period where your family issues become clouded with unrealistic, idealistic values. Be gentle with younger members, this is their natural default. You may be overly romantic at this time and need to keep one foot on the ground.

Saturday 26th

When the Moon sits with Pluto you may feel very powerful. However, this is also opposite Venus in your intimacy sector, and you may become manipulative or passive-aggressive. Be ever mindful of how you would like to be treated and don't overstep the mark if seeking to know someone better.

Sunday 27th

This is a difficult day and it's possible that you will see power plays and mind games. You are willing to fight for a cause today and may buy into conspiracy theories or join a revolution. Your energy is high thanks to Mars. Play by the rules and stay safe.

Monday 28th

Your emotions are high, and you are very verbose. You may need a soapbox for shouting your speeches and getting a wider audience. Family issues concern you later in the day and you may be loathe to change one role for another. You may wear many hats today.

Tuesday 29th

Make sure that you don't trip yourself up with idealistic thinking. Take the time to consider anything you've newly learned and if it is of any real value to you. You may be going along with the crowd and not singing your own song.

Wednesday 30th

As the Moon meets newly retrograde Neptune, you may have trouble separating fact from fiction. Your head may be full of new ideas and concepts but you cannot get them straight and clear. This is not possible right now and they're taking up room. Dismiss them and come back to them later.

JULY

. . . .

Thursday 1st

With both the Moon and Mars in fire signs you may feel like
you can run a marathon. However, this energy only serves
to get you through the day with energy to spare. You may
lock horns with an authority figure so be mindful in your
communications.

Friday 2nd

Everything appears to be on board for you to experience and
share creativity and your own self-expression. It's likely that
you are particularly articulate when speaking words of love.
Mercury is pleased by your eagerness to be your authentic self.
You're mindful of boundaries and make an impression on
someone important.

Saturday 3rd

You're more grounded and wish to experience activities that
take you back into your body. Earth energy allows you to get
out into nature and enjoy the natural world. You may be doing
a service to others which will take you outdoors. Host a dinner
party this evening.

Sunday 4th

Be careful out there today. Mars and Uranus are connecting
to the Moon and you may come across as stubborn. There's
potential for arguments and high tempers so you'll need to
steer clear of unnecessary drama. Avoid lovers' tiffs if you can
as they can be harsh.

Monday 5th

Get to grips with something that grounds you and brings you back into your body today. Neptune and Pluto connect to the Moon asking for a different perspective and change. What can you transform today? An opinion may be changed if you become more flexible in your thinking.

Tuesday 6th

The Moon drops into your relationship sector and once more you reach out to an unknown future. You may be stepping into a reality that's too far removed from your own and this will not do you any favours. Communicate your thoughts at all times to your lover. Keep them in the loop.

Wednesday 7th

Today is great for romantic gestures but you must remember to remain respectful. Don't try pushing boundaries or you'll spoil an otherwise perfect moment. The celestial lovers, Mars and Venus are getting closer in your travel sector. Why not plan an intimate trip for two?

Thursday 8th

Your head and heart are in sync as the Moon joins Mercury. You're not shy in asking for what you desire or expressing a wish to learn more about someone. This is one of those days where you're set on talking all day, just remember to listen too.

Friday 9th

The Moon flows through your intimacy sector picking up signals. Your own comfort and needs can be expressed now. You may wish to explore the depths of life with a certain person. Ensure that both of you can swim before dipping your toes in. This is a very deep sector.

Saturday 10th

There's a New Moon in your intimacy sector. This is a great opportunity to set intentions and goals with a lover. Define safety zones and discuss how you can protect one another without becoming smothering. Your relationships will deepen if you can nurture and nourish each other.

Sunday 11th

You bravely step up and face a person who is being bossy or obstructive towards you. This may be someone who is highly regarded such as a spiritual leader or an authority in your wider groups. Don't let them dull your shine and diminish you now. Be courageous and bold.

Monday 12th

Venus and Mars are getting closer and the Moon meets both today. This is an exceptionally good time to stand side by side with a lover and take a leap together into the unknown. Uranus is squaring off with the Moon meaning that you should expect the unexpected now.

Tuesday 13th

Mars and Venus meet. The celestial lovers enjoy their time together in your travel sector. This influence makes you want to explore the world and the foreign philosophies, cultures and religions it has to offer. More than that, you may have found the right person to do that with.

Wednesday 14th

Your efficient and methodical mind helps to keep you grounded while Venus and Mars are still dancing. This is great for browsing travel brochures and making lists of what you would like to do. You may now check your schedule and find the right time for an adventure with your partner.

Thursday 15th

Your dreams may be put on hold today by your mundane duties. You may come back to them at any time but work and your everyday chores must not be neglected. The Sun connects to Neptune and is burning away some of the illusions in order for you to see clearly.

Friday 16th

The weekend arrives and you need to balance your highly active heart and mind. Something as ordinary as a night out with friends can help you to remember the other good things in life. Your partner may need your attention, but you need to see your friends too today.

Saturday 17th

The Moon makes a connection to Mars and Venus. This can be great for friendship circles of all genders as you will get along very well. The polarities of male and female will make a great mix of fun. You may be partying all through the night, have fun.

Sunday 18th

The Moon in your hidden sector may unearth some of your deepest, darkest thoughts. If you feel the need to share, find someone who will not judge you. Uranus is opposite the Moon and this can make for earthquakes and tsunamis in your psyche. This can be uncomfortable so stay safe.

Monday 19th

You're dreaming of a near future and Pluto is supporting that dream as he believes it may be the transformation you need. The gold in your psyche is waiting to be found. It may be that you're finding a new part of yourself or revealing one that you have kept hidden.

Tuesday 20th

The Moon is in your sign. This gives you the confidence to express deeply held emotions and let hurtful ones go. Talk to people who don't shock easily. Get things off your chest, no matter how risqué or taboo they are.

Wednesday 21st

This is another day where the Moon makes great connections to Mars and Venus. This time, with the Moon in your sign, you can make it all about you without upsetting anyone. Your explorer, gypsy soul needs to be heard and validated. Look for documentaries or books to whet your appetite for the unknown.

Thursday 22nd

Venus leaves your travel sector as the Sun enters it. This will ensure that the warmth and love for new adventures persists. Venus will now help to bring in the finances needed as she sails through your career sector. The Sun is at home and will shine brightly on your travel plans.

Friday 23rd

The Moon meets with Pluto today. This always feels like a control issue regarding your self-worth for you. Stay calm, you may just need to check finances and assess what is valuable to you. You're not being threatened. The Moon's connection to Neptune is confusing you.

Saturday 24th

A Full Moon in your communications sector shows how you've been putting yourself out there to the wider world and getting involved. You may see a project come to completion now or experience a person in your wider groups in a different way. Communicate your security needs to others.

Sunday 25th

Today it's likely that you experience conflict or power struggles. There's difficult energy coming from the most disruptive of planets, Uranus, and the warrior Mars. You'll need to be careful of what you're saying as motor-mouth Mercury is opposing Pluto. You may be sharing too much personal information.

Monday 26th

This is another tricky day to navigate. Venus and the Moon are facing off and this feminine energy can be bitchy and nasty. Your career and home life are the subjects of the tension. Look at what patriarchal and matriarchal roles mean to you. How are they in conflict?

Tuesday 27th

The Moon meets Neptune. It's unlikely that you will get any clarity now. You may seem lost in a sea of fog with your family problems. You will need to ask for help and shout it very loudly. Those who wander through life aimlessly need a wake-up call.

Wednesday 28th

Mercury enters your travel sector which is great news as he will help you to make all the enquiries and get the information you need. The emotional Moon supports this from your creative sector as you express yourself clearly in order to get what you need to know.

Thursday 29th

Mars marches into your career sector. You'll be super-efficient at sorting the wheat from the chaff now. Any slackers will fall by the wayside as you're more assertive at work and others notice. You will have all the energy you need to get through a summer at work.

Friday 30th

As the Moon shifts into your health and duties sector, it immediately connects to Mars. This is the time to make solid plans and manifest them into reality. Mars will give you the drive to do so while the Moon keeps you emotionally invested. Onwards and upwards.

Saturday 31st

You may feel like you've hit a brick wall. Take a breather and recharge. You may have been overdoing it recently with Mars as your cheerleader. Back down and use the weekend to rest and recuperate. Your plans will still be there next week. Indulge in what you fancy today.

AUGUST

. . . .

Sunday 1st

Today you may feel anxious. Mercury is in the heart of the Sun and silent. Your job is to listen for messages, wisdom and advice. This is easier said than done as the Moon is with Uranus making you restless and unable to express yourself.

Monday 2nd

You can relax a little as you're drawn to talking with a lover or best friend who understands you. There may be friction going on with hostile communications, but you're able to detach and observe from a neutral place. Keeping your interactions simple will help.

Tuesday 3rd

Those ideas and plans for a future with a loved one enter your head again. You take joy in being able to express yourself and your vision. Speaking from your heart may come naturally and it will be surprising how open you are with people who are important to you.

Wednesday 4th

The jobs and commitments that you do each day now become a hindrance. You may be wondering how you can possibly fulfil your own dreams when you're relied on so much by others. You'll need to think this through on every level. You can do this.

. . . .

Thursday 5th

A deeply intimate Moon may influence your mood in a way that can make you defensive. You may be struggling to step out of a comfort zone but at the same time, you wish to explore strange topics that interest you. Stay rooted and reach out from your home base for now.

Friday 6th

You're sensitive but grounded. The Moon opposes Pluto and you may feel pressured to change or conform. This is a passing Moon phase. Look at your other feelings. You may realise that your work and commitments actually contribute to your sense of security.

Saturday 7th

This morning you're fierier and more optimistic. This is the Sagittarius people know. Other planetary influences are affecting the wider world around you, but you soldier on with a smile. Remember that a good base enables you to explore and come back when you need to retreat. You can do this.

Sunday 8th

A New Moon in your travel sector is the confirmation you need to set intentions, make plans and go. This fiery Moon lifts your spirits and enables you to be bold and courageous. You understand that there are some restrictions, but you now resolve to work around them.

Monday 9th

The Moon meets Mercury and your head and heart are in sync. You have a busy mind and your thoughts are following the trail of your heart and your soul's desires. An opposition to Jupiter, your ruler, keeps you realistic. Listen to any advice you're offered now as it will be valuable.

Tuesday 10th

Today may be tricky for you to navigate. The Moon meets Mars and you're energised and fired up to follow your dreams. However, your inner critic will fill you with doubts and you shrink back a little. Simply take a breather and aim for a subjective viewpoint.

Wednesday 11th

The Moon meets Venus and they have a chat. Venus says that you must take a brave step into the unknown and follow your soul's desires. You're supported in this. Take in all the information that comes your way and discuss it with your social groups. Weigh everything up.

Thursday 12th

Mercury is now in your career sector. He is your perfect ally and will help you to research, communicate and manage your work better than you already do. You will be noticed for your extra efforts. Venus and Pluto connect to help you make necessary changes that benefit you.

Friday 13th

Aim for balance and go with the natural flow of change and endings. This may be difficult but will ultimately be right for you. Your social circle calls you today. Finding time to be with your wider friendships may help to remind you what makes you happy outside of your personal dreams.

Saturday 14th

The Moon is in your hidden sector. You may spend a lot of time ruminating and trying to organise your thoughts. Mercury butts in to assist. Making a list will help. You may only be seeing obstructions right now and this makes your mood low.

Sunday 15th

Restless energy from Uranus only serves to make you feel that you're chained to your commitments. You may feel rebellious and start shouting or trying to break free. There's another way to do this. Listen to Pluto in your finance and values sector for ways to make responsible changes.

Monday 16th

As the Moon drops into your own sign, you may feel more empowered. Your words and actions may not match your feelings today, but you're listening to the advice of others. Venus enters your social sector and will spread the love around. Expect a lot of dining out with friends now.

Tuesday 17th

You may need to put something on hold as you look at it from a different perspective. Family issues arise and you need to factor these in with your hopes and dreams. Remember that Neptune is causing a fog here and so you will not be able to get a great deal of clarity.

Wednesday 18th

Thinking about your search for truth may make you a little rebellious. This is nothing new to you, but you may begin to disregard your previous belief system. The Moon in your values sector helps you to make responsible decisions and curb your rebel instincts.

Thursday 19th

The planet of disruption, Uranus, turns retrograde today. As he sits in your health and duties sector this may manifest as an illness that needs attention. Your mind is so busy that you're fit to burst and need an outlet. A lively discussion will help disperse some stress.

Friday 20th

The Sun sits opposite Jupiter. You may see a clash of egos. This could be between yourself and a person in authority or a spiritual leader. You will need to evaluate the things you do for yourself and what you do in groups for the benefit of the wider world.

Saturday 21st

Your conversations can be laced with irritability today as you don't seem to be getting through to people. Here is where you must start looking at your regular duties and commitments outside of your career. You may feel restricted and wish to run away from it all.

Sunday 22nd

A Full Moon in your communications sector has brought something to your attention now. You may now be seeing an interest group in a new light. Is it still serving you? Is it still of interest? You may find that you've outgrown certain people and groups. Let them go.

Monday 23rd

The Sun is now in your career sector. This will highlight the excellent work that you do. Your natural efficiency will be noticed, and you may be rewarded. You may feel drained today as the Moon opposes Mars. Take it slowly or use up your Mars energy at the gym.

Tuesday 24th

The Moon meets Neptune. You may wish to be reunited with your inner compass, but you may be led astray with fantasy thinking. Your mind chatter may be telling you to stay grounded, but you are enjoying the wistfulness of drifting right now. A fantasy novel will satisfy this urge.

Wednesday 25th

Your creative, romantic side comes out now and adds to the dreamy mood you're already in. This may be more melancholic than you would like but it's possible to create great art or poetry now. Channelling your mood this way helps you to see it objectively.

Thursday 26th

You now have too many projects on the go. You need to let something go or finish it up and move on. Say goodbye to interests that have become more of a bind than a joy. Free up some space for something new and worthwhile to enter your life.

Friday 27th

The Moon shifts and you're more grounded. Your daily duties keep you from being idealistic. Keep to your schedules and get through the day at a steady pace. This will give you some peace from the troubling thoughts and stress you've had recently. Good food and company will also help.

Saturday 28th

The Moon meets newly retrograde Uranus. Venus connects too and smooths over any niggles you may be having. A social event with friends can be lively and just what you need. Aligning your energy with Uranus and Mars can make restless energy into something spectacular and new.

Sunday 29th

Nice connections to the Moon mean that you can articulate feelings to others. Although they may not totally understand, you've let them know and this is a good start. Your family will be supportive and try to see your point of view. You may see some pressure eased now.

Monday 30th

Mercury enters your social sector. You may be doing new and interesting research. Your wider groups, including those on social media, may be picking up pace and taking you in a new direction. Perhaps this is what will take up the space you have recently made. New projects excite you.

Tuesday 31st

The Moon is in your relationship sector now. Although you normally enjoy this time, you may find that you're not as connected as you would like. Don't worry too much, this is a quickly passing phase. Keep conversation polite, respectful and minimal today. Try to be as clear as you can.

SEPTEMBER
· · · · · · · · · · · · · · · · ·

Wednesday 1st

Today is all about self-preservation. Console yourself with nurturing techniques such as favourite foods and films. Stick to the familiar and you cannot go wrong. Mercury is squaring off with the Moon so take the time and tune into your intuition instead. What does it tell you?

Thursday 2nd

Staying in your comfort zone will help to stabilise your emotions. Friends may try to drag you out for a social event, but you aren't interested. You may have a conflict between work and family commitments. Make a decision between getting the facts or allowing yourself to dream.

Friday 3rd

If you're comfortable in your environment, you're able to wander off with your thoughts. You may be contemplating deep issues such as the mysteries of death and rebirth. Pluto is nagging you. There's something that needs to die and be reborn anew. Do you know what it is?

Saturday 4th

Have you ever wanted to break free and start a new journey? Of course you have, you're the celestial explorer. Well today, the harsh connections from the Moon to Uranus and Saturn imply just that. You may be chomping at the bit and ready to leave now.

Sunday 5th

There may be a social event that you can tag along with today.
Check your friendship groups and look for a late Summer festival
or an open day for higher education. You're seeking a new path and
must be open-minded as it may not be in the direction you think.

Monday 6th

You may have some proof-reading to do. You're forced to slow
down and evaluate where you are now. Your rational mind is
needed as Pluto is nagging you again. Try to be detached and
unemotional if there's an ending or closure to be made.
This may be a friendship.

Tuesday 7th

A New Moon in your career sector is a golden opportunity to
take a brave new step up the corporate ladder. Mars is here
waiting for you to make a definitive move. Stay focused and
don't let your mind wander off into fantasy thinking.

Wednesday 8th

As the Moon settles into your social sector, you appear to get
help from an unlikely source. Check your inbox as there may be
something there which has been left unopened or overlooked.
Saturn, although retrograde, is asking you to consider and be
aware of how you communicate. Take responsibility and reply to
an invitation.

Thursday 9th

The Moon meets Mercury so expect a lot of head chatter or social
activity. Your online friends could be buzzing with excitement.
Many minds can come up with something new and innovative.
Join in the process and find clarity and balance there that you can
harness for yourself.

Friday 10th

The Moon and Venus meet up shortly before they both slip into your hidden sector. You will benefit from having some time to yourself and indulging in art, beauty and secret longings. Venus is quite the seductress here, you may be drawn into new territory now.

Saturday 11th

Uranus faces off with the Moon and you get that familiar restless urge to break free. Take note of how and why this triggers you every month. You may come up against someone important and find that you have to justify your own part in an unusual or controversial conversation.

Sunday 12th

This afternoon the Moon slips into your own sign and you have more confidence and optimism. You may be looking back at the past and renewing a skill or interest you once had. This may come in handy now. An elder or teacher may challenge you to think in a different way.

Monday 13th

If you need to get clear on an issue regarding family or your dreams and visions, ask your friendship groups. Mercury is sitting there just waiting to get stuck into a good conversation or line of inquiry. Your social groups may have just the collective wisdom you need right now.

Tuesday 14th

The Sun sits opposite Neptune and is burning away some of the mist. Keep your attention focused on the area surrounding family or your true north as you may get a glimpse of clarity. This afternoon you need to see to financial matters you may have overlooked recently.

Wednesday 15th

You have no time for idle chatter today. You must look at your commitments and decide which ones are dragging you down. It's time to lose any perceived chains and extra baggage. Aim high and take the first steps. Mars marches into your social sector, prepare for war.

Thursday 16th

Your emotions are in sync with your ego. You consider your career and how you can progress without stepping on anyone's toes. This may be added to your dream list and become a means to get you to other places in the world. Make calls and emails this afternoon.

Friday 17th

You're perfectly aware now of what needs to be decluttered from your life. The Sun connects to Pluto to show you how to make gold from dead weight. As the Moon meets Saturn, you understand that you've just learned an important life lesson, and it may be brutal.

Saturday 18th

This is a quiet day for you to enjoy catching up with people. The Moon meets Jupiter who acts as the law, the truth and spiritual advancement. Although still retrograde, you get support here. He will also give you more joy and motivation to see your visions manifested.

Sunday 19th

This may be a lovely family day which is enjoyable and simple. You take time to pause and reflect on the year gone by and how you've advanced. You may be whimsical and romantic. It's also likely that you shock people as you reveal some of your hidden sides.

Monday 20th

A bright Full Moon ends the day in your family sector. The Moon is pulling Neptune's tides and bringing your dreams ever closer to the shore. Change is happening whether you're instrumental or not. Go with the natural flow of things today but keep your life jacket on.

Tuesday 21st

Your energy picks up as the Moon enters your creative sector. You enjoy discussing your many plans and ideas and can articulate your reasons for these well. If you put these down on paper, in art or poetry they will form a natural dialogue of your growth process.

Wednesday 22nd

It's the Autumn Equinox and time to reflect on the outgoing, longer days. Give gratitude for the warmth and inspiration you've received. As the balance tips, you may find that you're more passive and receptive but still busy making plans for future times.

Thursday 23rd

You may find that today is a little tricky. It's likely that you express yourself in a way that reveals too much about your inner workings. Be careful who you share this with, as not everyone is as open-minded as you. Think before you speak or voice a radical opinion.

Friday 24th

Stress may give you a headache or minor health concern. You may feel like a volcano ready to blow and you may clash with an elder or boss figure. Lie low if you can and see to your regular duties. Make sure all chores are done then relax with good food and company.

Saturday 25th

Mercury retrograde will happen again from tomorrow. This will occur throughout your social sector so be sure to practice the pause before you respond to anything. Use today to back up your devices and double-check your travel plans. Be careful on the roads now.

Sunday 26th

As Mercury retrograde begins, the Moon enters your relationship sector. You have energy and a defined purpose to share with a loved one. Play by the rules and be respectful at all times. Remember not to overstep another's boundaries unless they invite you. Saturn and Mars can make you assertive today.

Monday 27th

You may need to listen to another point of view today. This may be difficult, and you will not quite be able to grasp it. Your mind is going over new things and processing the information, but Neptune's energy is keeping you in the dark for now. Return to it at another time.

Tuesday 28th

It's possible that you see the first effect of Mercury retrograde today. The Moon is connecting in a helpful way, but this means nothing right now. There may be a difference of opinion or a conflict of interests between your love relationship and your social groups.

Wednesday 29th

Mars and Uranus are combining to make you irritable. You're extra defensive and may need to retreat into your safety zone until this passes. Venus and Neptune together dredge up the self-serving parts of your psyche and you may be very selfish. This is fine if you are spoiling yourself with comfort foods.

Thursday 30th

There's a huge amount of water energy in the air today. This may feel threatening as water will put out your fire. However, you could put it to good use and reach out to connect or merge with others who share your values and beliefs.

OCTOBER

....

Friday 1st

You get some of your fire back today as the Moon drops into your travel sector. You're itching to get out and broaden your horizons. Look at breathing fresh life into your social groups. You may find that a new connection or invitation comes your way and excites your sense of adventure.

Saturday 2nd

Communications need to be measured and considered right now. You may be confronted with discussions that are multi-layered and complicated to understand. It's possible that you're pushy with your own opinion and stubborn when accepting another's. Hidden desires may be triggered and surface for healing.

Sunday 3rd

This morning you're in a steady, reliable and methodical mood. You may feel at a standstill but will work your way through this eventually. It will feel uncomfortable at first and you may have to deal with awkward people. Stay with the facts and you'll not go wrong.

Monday 4th

The Moon in your career sector helps you to stay grounded and on track. Uranus connects to nudge you out of a rut, and you may find the answer to a problem. It's tempting to drift off and ignore your duties, but you're professional and goal orientated.

Tuesday 5th

You may overindulge and buy something for the home which is frivolous and expensive. Ideas of decluttering or a total make-over have been milling around your head recently and you may have taken the plunge already. Clearing up a part of your life is satisfying.

Wednesday 6th

A New Moon in your social sector could be the start of a new way of relating to your wider groups. New energy comes in and excites you. Mars is connecting to make this Moon driven and assertive. Perhaps your groups are onto something big. Pluto also turns direct.

Thursday 7th

The harmonising Moon squares off with Pluto. Change is afoot whether you like it or not. There's much discussion, thought and research going on. You may like to join an activist movement which will bring about a much-needed change. The Moon enters your hidden sector just as Venus leaves it.

Friday 8th

The Sun and Mars are sitting together in your social sector. This is a time of high activity where egos may clash or combine to get things shifted. A rebellion may start now. The Moon in your hidden sector is rousing feelings you would usually keep you yourself.

Saturday 9th

Your emotions are focused on yourself as the Moon drops into your own sign and meets Venus. Putting yourself first is important now. No more accepting things and people who aren't good for you. Mercury and Mars meet too. Expect a lot of words and action that comes from the heart.

Sunday 10th

Saturn turns direct in your communications sector. The shackles are off and you can preach from your soapbox. It's likely that his retrograde taught you a thing or two about getting the right audience and being mindful when speaking. You're a force to be reckoned with now.

Monday 11th

You must put your own opinions to one side and listen carefully to the advice from an elder, leader or spiritual person. This will stand you in good stead in the near future. Jupiter, your ruler, is connecting to the Moon and has an important message for you.

Tuesday 12th

A gentle day comes as a relief to you. The Moon in your finance sector connects to Uranus so it's possible that you make an impulse buy. You may also see a new way to get through your mundane duties which will reap benefits in the long term.

Wednesday 13th

You're getting closer to your true north but still need to clear the decks and make space. Start by listening to Venus who want you to feel good about change. Letting something go need not be a heartache if it's done with love and compassion.

Thursday 14th

In your communications sector, the Moon meets newly direct Saturn. This may manifest as a meeting with a teacher or elder where you have to justify your recent actions. Open your mind, a fresh new lesson is about to start, and it comes from a brand new you.

Friday 15th

To verify Saturn's lessons, the Moon now meets Jupiter. Your ruler will turn direct this week but needs to ensure that your adventurous soul is ready. Truth and only truth will be acceptable now. You must throw away false teachings and flaky philosophies and make your own way.

Saturday 16th

Spending time with your tribe will be a pleasant activity this weekend. The Moon supports this with soft energy as you merge and connect with your loved ones. Simply allow yourself to go with the tides and appreciate the beauty of family. Celebrate the diversity within your family unit.

Sunday 17th

As the Moon meets Neptune and you enjoy detaching from problems, Jupiter turns direct. Your ruler blesses you with his gifts of optimism and joy. This can be a day where everyone chips in and gets a chore done or alternatively a family event becomes a party. Expect the surprises today.

Monday 18th

Mercury turns direct. The pressure is lifting from your communications and social sectors. If you have put off signing a contract or making a travel plan, rest assured that you can now revisit these and forge ahead. This afternoon gives you the energy and motivation to soldier on.

Tuesday 19th

Your creative sector hosts the Moon and you're high-spirited. The future is clearer, and plans can be restarted. Mars is connecting to your ruler and you have the go-ahead to express yourself at all levels. Venus wishes you to speak from the heart and ask for what you desire now.

Wednesday 20th

There's a Full Moon in your creative sector. You may see something come to completion. A love affair is highlighted, as are children. It's possible that you're overwhelmed with something and your energy is drained as Mars is opposing the Moon.

Thursday 21st

You may come across a small stumbling block which will fuel your temper very quickly. This will feel like you've only just begun something on a high note and instantly you have run into problems. Stay calm, this isn't as bad as you first think it is.

Friday 22nd

Don't give up at the first hurdle. You have a moment where you just want to switch off and forget about everything. You're being hard on yourself and over-exaggerating the situation. This is a passing phase and will be over quickly. Don't jeopardise your potential now.

Saturday 23rd

If it's possible, spend today with someone who knows and understands you very well. You may wish to think and ruminate out loud. Thrashing out ideas and feelings about something with a lover may help to give you a better perspective. The Sun enters and illuminates your hidden sector.

. . . .

Sunday 24th

The one thing you mustn't forget to do is to express your own needs. The Moon sits opposite Venus and you may be inclined to go along with another even if you don't feel right about it. Mercury is allowing you to speak freely with your social groups.

Monday 25th

Your dreams and visions might not be accessible to you but that doesn't stop you from discussing them. You may be overly assertive and feel self-righteous. Be careful that you don't brag or become a bore. Say your piece but prepare to hear another.

Tuesday 26th

You're emotionally inclined to think deeply and intensely today. It's likely that you cannot emotionally detach from your opinions. You may be defensive and protective of your own home, money and belief systems. Take some time alone today and recharge your batteries as you may be emotionally drained.

Wednesday 27th

The Moon opposes Pluto and that familiar nagging for change returns. You aren't ready to do this right now. Stay inside your comfort zone and don't let yourself be bullied or manipulated. You may need to switch off and close down again. See to your own emotional needs first.

Thursday 28th

Venus and Jupiter connect to make it possible for you to express yourself clearly. The Moon in your travel sector makes you outgoing and courageous. Short bursts are better than sustained effort today. Speak your mind truthfully then agree to draw a line under it for the sake of your energy.

Friday 29th

You must be very careful not to keep blowing your own trumpet today. Uranus the disruptor is connecting to the Moon and you may be so emotionally charged that you blow up in volcanic proportions. Surround yourself with your wider friendship groups and gather advice and wisdom.

Saturday 30th

Mars enters your hidden sector. This will have the effect of you being ruthless and brutal with your inner work. You may be very hard on yourself. The Sun is squaring off with Saturn which also confirms that you're working hard to bring out your shadow and heal it.

Sunday 31st

Concern yourself with daily chores as it will help take your mind off deeper issues. Take a break from the intense and do mundane work. Go through a messy drawer, do some admin or check your planner and schedules. Add some dates to your diary for treat times.

NOVEMBER
·················

Monday 1st

Today you may be trying to achieve harmony between your work and home life. You get an idea of changes to be made and how you might do this comfortably. Mercury helps you to think about which contacts are good for you and will help you grow.

Tuesday 2nd

Your social network takes up your mind and heart space. The Moon meets the point of destiny and you're pulled towards making choices which will feed your soul. New and exciting cause stimulate your need to do something worthwhile for the greater good of the wider world.

Wednesday 3rd

You have a heart to heart with yourself and you may try separating logic from emotion. This is not easy to do. Pluto is still asking for you to end something and this could be a project you have a lot of emotional investment in. You will find a way in time.

Thursday 4th

The Moon enters your hidden sector and meets Mars. You may feel some anxiety and tension. This will become a Full Moon and give you some insight or deeper introspection. This is likely to be uncomfortable so take time to process these new feelings and epiphanies.

Friday 5th

There's a lot of highly charged energy for you to deal with.
The Sun in your hidden sector antagonises Uranus. You may
see shadow material surfacing and experience many triggers.
Mercury enters your private hidden sector. This will help you
to dig as deep as you need to find the answers.

Saturday 6th

The Moon enters your sign and your emotions settle down
a little. Venus is in your finance and values sector and making a
great connection to Mercury. Between the two of them, they will
ensure that you understand your self-worth and the process of
healing you are going through.

Sunday 7th

You might feel that you have lost sight of your dreams. Your
inner compass does not seem to be calibrated very well. Your
ruler, Jupiter, asks that you stay positive and look at things
from a different angle, just for today. How does it feel to
observe yourself from the outside?

Monday 8th

Doing the hard work of introspection is beginning to pay off.
It's likely that you've surprised yourself with how much you've
learned about your inner defaults already. Mars is driving you
on and Mercury is sharing the information he finds with you.

Tuesday 9th

The Moon meets Pluto. You have a chance to recycle
something or put it in the refuse bin once and for all. This may
be a positive death and rebirth of values you once lived by and
have now realised don't serve you anymore. Well done.

Wednesday 10th

Mercury and Mars meet up and become a source of strength to you. Saturn is watching how you deal with situations that may require you to be Saturn-like. You will need to be firm and fair and put healthy boundaries in place to protect your energy and vulnerability right now.

Thursday 11th

The Moon in your communications sector meets Jupiter. Recent feelings may now feel bigger and ready to burst. You're ready for these to be exposed. Speaking your truth may upset someone or interrupt your daily routine. This will be brief, and you can deal with it easily.

Friday 12th

Today the Sun makes a connection to Neptune that helps you see things with a little more clarity. The whole picture will not be revealed just yet, but some of the fog is lifting. This will make you pause and take note before you proceed any further. Venus will bring you balance.

Saturday 13th

Let the Moon guide you into enjoying some family time. With your tribe, you may be able to align your inner compass once more. Listen to your heart as the Moon meets Neptune. Be still and patient. Refrain from spilling your secrets today as this could have unwanted effects.

Sunday 14th

You're much blessed as the Sun and Moon are in sync. Your ego and conscious mind are in touch with your emotions and you feel happy. This afternoon your creative side comes out and you're able to reach out to others and be an example to them.

Monday 15th

Don't let anything knock you back. It may be that you've come across an obstruction or unforeseen problem. Talk to people about this, don't try solving it on your own as you will become frustrated. You need help from a professional or someone in your wider groups.

Tuesday 16th

Weird energy has you thinking about endings and beginnings but in different ways. The Sun in your hidden sector may make you feel ready for action, but the Moon has an emotional connection that you're not ready to cut just yet. Take note of how this is triggering you and sleep on it.

Wednesday 17th

The Moon shifts into your health and duties sector. This time of the month is useful if you need to distract yourself from deeper issues. However, Mars in your hidden sector is facing off with Uranus and that can only mean trouble. Stress may get to you.

Thursday 18th

The best thing you can do today is to lie low. If it's possible, speak to no-one and stay home protecting your energy. Pick up a fantasy novel or binge watch a TV show. The planetary energy is far too unstable and can tip you over the edge. Stay safe.

Friday 19th

A Full Moon in your heath and duties sector may be the culmination of a health problem. This is like a spotlight on how you get through your day and how much you look after yourself. You may have experienced burn out. Venus tries to soothe you today, allow her to do so.

Saturday 20th

You need a close friend or lover to talk to this weekend. It will be helpful for you to simply talk and talk. You need to be heard and validated. Find someone with whom you can reveal your darker sides and not be judged. There are things you need to share now.

Sunday 21st

If today feels like you have lost your way again, be assured that this is just a quickly passing Moon phase. Be good to yourself and breathe deeply. A lover or best friend may have remedies or solutions that are new and useful for you. Talking therapy is the best.

Monday 22nd

The Sun enters your sign, so this is your birthday month. Happy Birthday! Venus and Mars are making a good connection enabling you to find the warrior heart within you. You will do the right thing and make plenty of time for yourself now.

Tuesday 23rd

The Moon and Venus are opposing each other, and you have guilty feelings about being too self-indulgent. This is not the case, you're currently doing a lot of deep work and this needs time and self-love. Carry on doing the right thing for you.

Wednesday 24th

Mercury is finishing up his time in your psyche. It's crucial now that you take care of all the pearls he has discovered in your darkest places. His underworld research has brought you information that you can throw to Pluto the next time he asks.

Thursday 25th

Mercury enters your sign and meets the point of past lessons. This is a great opportunity to let him drop something in there and let it go for good. Mars and Venus are supporting this and giving you masculine strength and feminine compassion to lovingly release some baggage.

Friday 26th

Today you're brave and outgoing. Slight reservations prevent you from being the truth-seeking Sagittarius you are, but your optimism still shines through. You may wish to look at some study options which will help with your soul work and bring you into touch with like-minded people.

Saturday 27th

Your sense of calm returns and you're much more centred. Mercury has unearthed your treasure, shown it to you and discarded the waste. Today you may think about a thorough detox of your body and mind. A spiritual retreat or group could do wonders for you. Try meditation or yoga too.

Sunday 28th

The Moon opposes Neptune and you defer from entering the fantasy world he is offering. Stay on task as you declutter and cleanse yourself. You may have a revelation or two as you do so. Good food and company can help to keep you grounded.

Monday 29th

Mercury is silent in your own sign. Remain centred and listen to his messages. Your social groups may now offer a way that you can achieve your soul desires. Mars is still the driving force in your psyche and connects to Neptune to recalibrate your inner compass.

Tuesday 30th

Today there is lovely energy for you to access and work with. Venus and Neptune connect to show you the true value in your personal quest. Mercury and the Sun are receiving a lesson from Saturn. Your ego and essence are becoming more authentic as you learn more about your inner workings. Well done, this is fantastic.

DECEMBER

· · · · · · · · · · · · · · · · ·

Wednesday 1st

Neptune turns direct. Finally, you'll be able to grasp hold of your inner compass and let it guide you. The Moon dips into your hidden sector and you may find that you're looking around there and evaluating the job Mercury has just facilitated for you.

Thursday 2nd

Today may give you a test of some kind. The Moon sits opposite the disruptive Uranus and you may resent any or all things that appear to obstruct your dreams and visions. Sit tight and bite your lip, this will pass as quickly as it has come up.

Friday 3rd

When the Moon meets Mars in your hidden sector you become fiercely protective of your private life. This could cause you to detach and refuse to listen to important people. You may now begin to do things simply for the sake of not conforming to others' expectations of you.

Saturday 4th

A New Moon arrives in your sign. This will give you the green light you've been seeking to go ahead and follow your heart. Mercury gives you the itinerary and map. You already have the compass. Play by the rules and you won't fail. Set all your personal goals now.

Sunday 5th

Jupiter has a say now. He connects to the Moon in a helpful way and fills you with optimism and motivation. There's much for you to learn, discover and experience. Keep your fire alive as it's your driving force. Keep your eyes on the goal.

Monday 6th

The Moon is in your finance and values sector. You might find that you turn to the financial aspect of attaining your goals. Mars and Pluto assist with this as they are both concerned with money. Be studious and leave no stone unturned. Be responsible and think before you act.

Tuesday 7th

Pluto hosts the Moon and you may be looking at taxes, bank accounts or regular subscriptions. There may be some that are out of date or due for renewal. A back-up of resources may be required and is highly recommended. Make the necessary enquiries this afternoon.

Wednesday 8th

Be very patient. Once again you may find that there are obstacles in your way. Mars and Uranus are making you irritable and you're likely to throw a tantrum. Take it easy and ask around, there are others out there who can offer words of wisdom without you having to rebel.

Thursday 9th

It's time that you looked at the legalities of your dreams. Jupiter reminds you that law and order are part of the truth you desire. Let nothing trip you up. Stay calm. This afternoon you may be more idealistic. Keep one foot on the ground if you can.

Friday 10th

Today you may get a surprising piece of support from a family member. An innovative way of solving a problem may come to you and you make a small breakthrough. You're more open to advice so listen well, as it may come from an unlikely source.

Saturday 11th

The Moon meets Neptune as Venus meets Pluto. This influence will serve you very well. You're focused on your dreams and visions and able to factor in the financial consequences. Venus also helps to make any change go the way you desire. You may feel a major shift.

Sunday 12th

Get your creative juices flowing as there's something that needs your attention. You may be asked your unique opinion on something and the ideas come flowing freely. Venus and Pluto are still together bringing in the money and letting unnecessary things go. This is all good energy.

Monday 13th

Two planets change signs. Mercury enters your finance and values sector and becomes your money manager. Watch what is offered to you now. Mars enters your sign and will give you all the fire you need to march your way into your future. Buying and selling may be an option.

Tuesday 14th

You may have a moment where you're not looking after number one today. This may derail you a little. However, as the Moon enters your health and duties sector it gets easier to ask for what you want. A reshuffle of your duties may be in order now.

Wednesday 15th

The Moon meets Uranus and you could be in for a surprise. This could be a visit from a ghost of the past. Saturn is watching to see if your personal boundaries are strong and healthy enough to deal with this in a respectful manner.

Thursday 16th

After a small hiccup, you're back on track and making changes, clearing the decks and putting yourself first. The weekend is lining up for some time with a lover or best friend. Prepare now and get all your chores out of the way. You'll want to free up plenty of time.

Friday 17th

You're in the mood to talk until the wee hours. Pick your partner and enjoy time together or an early festive celebration. Mars in your sign sits opposite the Moon and you may be energised enough to dance or talk all night. Make sure that your partner is too.

Saturday 18th

Venus will turn retrograde today. This is a period of forty days in which you could possibly see an ex-lover return, relationships end or a lack of self-care. As she is in your finance and values sector it will likely manifest as money problems or low self-esteem.

Sunday 19th

A Full Moon hangs in your relationship sector and connects to your ruler. This is beneficial for lovers and those who like to learn, study and share their understanding. What did you begin in this area six months ago? Has something come to fruition now? You're protective of your relationships this evening.

Monday 20th

As the festive season arrives, take some time to gather in your favourite foods and activities. Mothers and fathers play a big role. Look at your defence mechanisms as they may trigger some unnecessary feelings in you. You may be told off like a child today.

Tuesday 21st

Today's the Winter Solstice. The longest night serves to remind you to give gratitude for the long days and to preserve your energy throughout the winter months. You may see a power struggle or some miscommunication. Enjoy the solstice fire energy now as it suits your outgoing manner.

Wednesday 22nd

The Sun settles into your finance and value sector. This will help you to see where you sometimes undervalue yourself. Remember this when Venus retrograde effect comes upon you. You are worthy of receiving grace and must keep your fire burning to guide others. The only way is up.

Thursday 23rd

Jupiter is saying goodbye to your communications sector. He will now spend a whole year bringing luck, joy and optimism to your family. Step into this next year with your ruler acting as Santa Claus and bestowing his good cheer all around. Christmas has come early for you and your tribe.

Friday 24th

You may need to get your serious mind working today. The Moon passes into your career sector and this is where you are methodical, meticulous and do everything by the rules. You will see tension building around you, but this is natural. Take the lead if you must.

Saturday 25th

Venus has retrograded back to meet Pluto. This festive day will not be without some power struggles and manipulation. You have likely overspent and it has come back to haunt you. Forget about your personal dreams today, go with the flow and join in the collective family dream.

Sunday 26th

You have complete control over the festive proceedings. You may even be hosting them. This afternoon, however, you're more inclined to spread some cheer with your social groups, even if it's just online. You tell a family member or two about your new goals and have a pleasant time doing so.

Monday 27th

Today the major rush of the season is feeling more balanced. You still have energy and can compensate for older family members and friends who have run out of steam. Be respectful and helpful to those who may need you to do odd jobs or simply require your presence.

Tuesday 28th

You may start to feel the strain. It's possible that you experience that ghost from the past re-entering your life. It's tempting to renew this connection, but you must have a serious think about it first. What can it offer you? Why did it leave you before, and what has changed to bring it back? Do this when the Moon enters your hidden sector tonight.

Wednesday 29th

Today is another test for you. The Moon opposes Uranus who is upsetting things in your health and duties sector. It's possible that you see a minor health problem after overdoing the festive treats. You will need to slow down. Detach and take time alone if you need to.

Thursday 30th

When you're alone, you secretly delight in the achievements of this year. You've worked hard and you are pleased with the results you have seen. Mercury has met Pluto for the first time since he was in your psyche and today he's disposing of the last of the garbage. See if you can feel this release and watch it go with love and compassion.

Friday 31st

The Moon is in your sign and you will be the life and soul
of any New Year's Eve party. Mars gives you the energy you
need for a fun time. Say goodbye to this year and give thanks
for the lessons it has brought you. Then celebrate all you
have accomplished and all you have to look forward to in the
coming year.

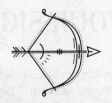

Sagittarius

....

PEOPLE WHO SHARE
YOUR SIGN

PEOPLE WHO
SHARE YOUR SIGN
. . . .

The free spirits of the zodiac can be easy to identify with their expansive thinking and lively approach to life. From Winston Churchill to Nicki Minaj, it feels like these inspiring Sagittarians where placed on Earth to motivate the masses. Whether this dual sign is influenced more by their intellectual mind or their physical strength, Sagittarians' daring attitudes will see them go far. Discover which of these optimistic Sagittarians share your exact birthday and see if you can spot the similarities.

November 23rd
Alexis Ren (1996), Miley Cyrus (1992), Snooki (1987), Kelly Brook (1979), Zoë Ball (1970), Vincent Cassel (1966), Nicolás Maduro, Venezuelan President (1962), John Schnatter (1961), Ludovico Einaudi (1955)

November 24th
Sarah Hyland (1990), Katherine Heigl (1978), Colin Hanks (1977), Stephen Merchant (1974), Shirley Henderson (1965), Billy Connolly (1942), Dale Carnegie (1888), Henri de Toulouse-Lautrec (1864)

November 25th
Katie Cassidy (1986), Gaspard Ulliel (1984), Joel Kinnaman (1979), Christina Applegate (1971), John F. Kennedy Jr. (1960), Ben Stein (1944), Ricardo Montalbán (1920), Karl Benz (1844)

November 26th

Rita Ora (1990), Danny Welbeck (1990), Tamsin Egerton (1988), Chris Hughes (1983), DJ Khaled (1975), Peter Facinelli (1973), Tina Turner (1939), Charles M. Schulz (1922)

November 27th

Professor Green (1983), Robin Givens (1964), Yulia Tymoshenko, Ukrainian Prime Minister (1960), William Fichtner (1956), Jil Sander (1943), Manolo Blahnik (1942), Jimi Hendrix (1942), Bruce Lee (1940)

November 28th

Karen Gillan (1987), Trey Songz (1984), Mary Elizabeth Winstead (1984), Daniel Henney (1979), Jon Stewart (1962), Martin Clunes (1961), Alfonso Cuarón (1961), Judd Nelson (1959), Ed Harris (1950), Friedrich Engels (1820)

November 29th

Diego Boneta (1990), Lauren German (1978), Chadwick Boseman (1977), Anna Faris (1976), Ryan Giggs (1973), Don Cheadle (1964), Jacques Chirac, French President (1932), Jackie Stallone (1921), C. S. Lewis (1898)

November 30th

Kaley Cuoco (1985), Chrissy Teigen (1985), Elisha Cuthbert (1982), Steve Aoki (1977), Ben Stiller (1965), Gary Lineker (1960), Billy Idol (1955), Ridley Scott (1937), Winston Churchill (1874), Lucy Maud Montgomery (1874), Mark Twain (1835)

December 1st

Chanel Iman (1990), Zoë Kravitz (1988), Vance Joy (1987), Janelle Monáe (1985), Sarah Silverman (1970), Pablo Escobar (1949), Bette Midler (1945), Woody Allen (1935)

December 2nd

Charlie Puth (1991), Alfred Enoch (1988), Teairra Marí (1987), Action Bronson (1983), Aaron Rodgers (1983), Britney Spears (1981), Nelly Furtado (1978), Lucy Liu (1968)

December 3rd

Amanda Seyfried (1985), Dascha Polanco (1982), Jenna Dewan (1980), Holly Marie Combs (1973), Brendan Fraser (1968), Daryl Hannah (1960), Julianne Moore (1960), Ozzy Osbourne (1948)

December 4th

Niykee Heaton (1994), Tyra Banks (1973), Kevin Sussman (1970), Jay-Z (1969), Fred Armisen (1966), Marisa Tomei (1964), Jeff Bridges (1949), Albert Bandura (1925)

December 5th

Anthony Martial (1995), Frankie Muniz (1985), Ronnie O'Sullivan (1975), Paula Patton (1975), Eddie the Eagle (1963), King Bhumibol the Great of Thailand (1927), Walt Disney (1901), Werner Heisenberg (1901)

December 6th

Stefanie Scott (1996), Alberto Contador (1982), Noel Clarke (1975), Sarah Rafferty (1972), Judd Apatow (1967), Nick Park (1958), Peter Buck (1956), Agnes Moorehead (1900)

December 7th

Nicholas Hoult (1989), Emily Browning (1988), Aaron Carter (1987), Dan Bilzerian (1980), John Terry (1980), Sara Bareilles (1979), Jennifer Carpenter (1979), Noam Chomsky (1928)

December 8th

AnnaSophia Robb (1993), Amir Khan (1986), Nicki Minaj (1982), Ian Somerhalder (1978), Dominic Monaghan (1976), Sinéad O'Connor (1966), Teri Hatcher (1964), Kim Basinger (1953), John Banville (1945)

December 9th

Simon Helberg (1980), Jesse Metcalfe (1978), Kurt Angle (1968), Felicity Huffman (1962), Donny Osmond (1957), John Malkovich (1953), Dame Judi Dench (1934), Kirk Douglas (1916)

December 10th

Teyana Taylor (1990), Gonzalo Higuaín (1987), Kim Sears (1987), Raven-Symoné (1985), Emmanuelle Chriqui (1975), Susanna Reid (1970), Kenneth Branagh (1960), Michael Clarke Duncan (1957), Emily Dickinson (1830)

December 11th

Hailee Steinfeld (1996), Mos Def (1973), Mo'Nique (1967), DJ Yella (1967), Marco Pierre White (1961), Nikki Sixx (1958), Jermaine Jackson (1954), Pranab Mukherjee, Indian President (1935)

December 12th

Yuvraj Singh (1981), Mayim Bialik (1975), Mädchen Amick (1970), Jennifer Connelly (1970), Regina Hall (1970), Sheila E. (1957), Bill Nighy (1949), Frank Sinatra (1915), Edvard Munch (1863)

December 13th

Katherine Schwarzenegger (1989), Taylor Swift (1989), Amy Lee (1981), Tom DeLonge (1975), Jamie Foxx (1967), Steve Buscemi (1957), Christopher Plummer (1929), Dick Van Dyke (1925)

December 14th

Tori Kelly (1992), Vanessa Hudgens (1988), Michael Owen (1979), Miranda Hart (1972), Natascha McElhone (1969), Dilma Rousseff, Brazilian President (1947), Jane Birkin (1946), Stan Smith (1946), B. K. S. Iyengar (1918), King George VI of the United Kingdom (1895)

December 15th

Jesse Lingard (1992), Keylor Navas (1986), Camilla Luddington (1983), Charlie Cox (1982), Michelle Dockery (1981), Adam Brody (1979), Don Johnson (1949), Tim Conway (1933), Gustave Eiffel (1832)

. . . .

December 16th

Zara Larsson (1997), Anna Popplewell (1988), Theo James (1984), Danielle Lloyd (1983), Krysten Ritter (1981), Miranda Otto (1967), Benjamin Bratt (1963), Philip K. Dick (1928), Wassily Kandinsky (1866)

December 17th

Dynamo (1982), Katheryn Winnick (1977), Milla Jovovich (1975), Sarah Paulson (1974), Giovanni Ribisi (1974), Rian Johnson (1973), Eugene Levy (1946), Muhammadu Buhari, Nigerian President (1942), Pope Francis (1936)

December 18th

Ashley Benson (1989), Christina Aguilera (1980), Katie Holmes (1978), Sia Furler (1975), DMX (1970), Brad Pitt (1963), Jonathan Cainer (1957), Ray Liotta (1954), Steven Spielberg (1946), Keith Richards (1943), J. J. Thomson (1856)

December 19th

Alexis Sánchez (1988), Karim Benzema (1987), Jake Gyllenhaal (1980), Alyssa Milano (1972), Tyson Beckford (1970), Richard Hammond (1969), Jennifer Beals (1963), Til Schweiger (1963), Maurice White (1941), Édith Piaf (1915)

December 20th

JoJo (1990), Bugzy Malone (1990), Bob Morley (1984), Jonah Hill (1983), Lara Stone (1983), Ashley Cole (1980), Chris Robinson (1966), Jenny Agutter (1952), Uri Geller (1946), Peter Criss (1945)

December 21st

Steven Yeun (1983), Tom Payne (1982), Emmanuel Macron, French President (1977), Kiefer Sutherland (1966), Ray Romano (1957), Jane Kaczmarek (1955), Chris Evert (1954), Samuel L. Jackson (1948), Jane Fonda (1937), Phil Donahue (1935)